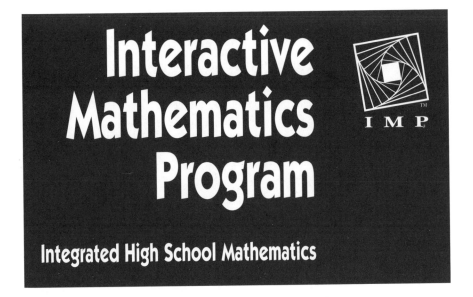

Interactive Mathematics Program

Integrated High School Mathematics

IMP

YEAR 1

Shadows

Dan Fendel and Diane Resek
with
Lynne Alper and Sherry Fraser

KEY CURRICULUM PRESS
Innovators in Mathematics Education

This material is based upon work
supported by the
National Science Foundation
under award number
ESI-9255262. Any opinions,
findings, and conclusions or
recommendations expressed
in this publication are those of
the authors and do not necessarily
reflect the views of the
National Science Foundation.

™ Interactive Mathematics Program,
IMP, and the IMP logo are trademarks
of Key Curriculum Press.

Key Curriculum Press
P.O. Box 2304
Berkeley, California 94702
editorial@keypress.com
http://www.keypress.com

10 9 8 7 6 5 4 3   00 99 98 97
ISBN 1-55953-255-6
Printed in the
United States of America

Project Editor
Casey FitzSimons

Additional Editorial Development
Dan Bennett, Bill Finzer, Crystal Mills

Editorial Production
Caroline Ayres, Debbie Cogan,
Greer Lleuad, Jason Luz

Editorial Assistants
Jeff Gammon, Romy Snyder

Teacher Reviews
Dave Calhoun, John Chart, Dwight Fuller,
Donna Gaarder, Dan Johnson, Jean Klanica,
Cathie Thompson

Multicultural Reviews
Edward Castillo, Ph.D., Sonoma State University
Genevieve Lau, Ph.D., Skyline College

Cover and Interior Design
Terry Lockman
Lumina Designworks

Cover Photography and Cover Illustration
Hillary Turner and Tom Fowler

Production
Luis Shein

Production Coordination
Susan Parini

Technical Graphics
Greg Reeves

Illustration
Tom Fowler, Evangelia Philippidis,
Diane Varner, Martha Weston,
April Goodman Willy

Publisher
Steven Rasmussen

Editorial Director
John Bergez

Acknowledgments

Many people have contributed to the development of the IMP curriculum, including the hundreds of teachers and many thousands of students who used preliminary versions of the materials. Of course, there is no way to thank all of them individually, but the IMP directors want to give some special acknowledgments.

We want to give extraordinary thanks to the following people who played unique roles in the development of the curriculum.

- **Bill Finzer** was one of the original directors of IMP before going on to different pastures. He helped shape the overall vision of the program, and worked on drafts of several Year 1 units.

- **Matt Bremer** did the initial revision of every unit after its pilot testing. Each unit of the curriculum also underwent extensive focus group reexamination after being taught for several years, and Matt did the rewrite of many units following the focus groups. He has read every word of everyone else's revisions as well, and has contributed tremendous insight through his understanding of high school students and the high school classroom.

- **Mary Jo Cittadino** became a high school student once again during the piloting of the curriculum, attending class daily and doing all the class activities, homework, and POWs. Because of this experience, her contributions to focus groups had a unique perspective. This is a good place to thank her also for her contributions to IMP as Network Coordinator for California. In that capacity, she has visited many IMP classrooms and answered thousands of questions from parents, teachers, and administrators.

- **Lori Green** left the classroom as a regular teacher after the 1989–90 school year and became a traveling resource for IMP classroom teachers. In that role, she has seen more classes using the curriculum than we can count, and the insights from her classroom observations have been a valuable resource in her work in the focus groups.

- **Celia Stevenson** developed the charming and witty graphics that graced the pre-publication versions of all the IMP units.

Several people played particular roles in the development of this unit, *Shadows:*

- Matt Bremer, Janice Bussey, Donna Gaarder, Lori Green, and Tom Zimmerman helped us create the version of *Shadows* that was pilot tested during 1989–90. They not only taught the unit in their classrooms that year, but also read and commented on early drafts, tested out almost all the activities during workshops that preceded the teaching, and then came back after teaching the unit with insights that contributed to the initial revision.

- Dean Ballard, Peter Herreshoff, and Melody Martinez joined Matt Bremer, Mary Jo Cittadino, and Lori Green for the focus group on *Shadows* in February, 1994. Their contributions built on several years of IMP teaching, including at least two years teaching this unit, and their work led to the development of the last field-test version of the unit.

- Dan Branham, Dave Calhoun, John Chart, Steve Hansen, Mary Hunter, Caran Resciniti, Gwennyth Trice, and Julie Walker field tested the post-focus group version of *Shadows* during 1994–95. Dave and John met with us when the teaching of the unit was finished to share their experiences. Their feedback helped shape the final version that now appears.

In creating this program, we needed help in many dimensions other than writing curriculum and giving support to teachers.

The National Science Foundation has been the primary sponsor of the Interactive Mathematics Program. We want to thank NSF for its ongoing support, and especially want to extend our personal thanks to Dr. Margaret Cozzens, Director of NSF's Division of Elementary, Secondary, and Informal Education, for her encouragement and her faith in our efforts.

We also want to acknowledge here the initial support for curriculum development from the California Postsecondary Education Commission and the San Francisco Foundation, and the major support for dissemination from the Noyce Foundation and the David and Lucile Packard Foundation.

Keeping all of our work going required the help of a first-rate office staff. This group of talented and hard-working individuals worked tirelessly on many tasks, such as sending out units, keeping the books balanced, helping us get our message out to the public, and handling communications with schools, teachers, and administrators. We greatly appreciate their dedication.

- Barbara Ford—Secretary

- Tony Gillies—Project Manager

- Marianne Smith—Publicist

- Linda Witnov—Outreach Coordinator

We want to thank Dr. Norman Webb, of the Wisconsin Center for Education Research, for his leadership in our evaluation program, and our Evaluation Advisory Board, whose expertise was so valuable in that aspect of our work.

- David Clarke, University of Melbourne

- Robert Davis, Rutgers University

- George Hein, Lesley College

- Mark St. John, Inverness Research Associates

Finally, we want to thank Steve Rasmussen, President of Key Curriculum Press, Casey FitzSimons, Key's Project Editor for the IMP curriculum, and the many others at Key whose work turned our ideas and words into published form.

Dan Fendel   Diane Resek   Lynne Alper   Sherry Fraser

The Interactive Mathematics Program

What is the Interactive Mathematics Program?

The Interactive Mathematics Program (IMP) is a growing collaboration of mathematicians, teacher-educators, and teachers who have been working together since 1989 on both curriculum development and teacher professional development.

What is the IMP curriculum?

IMP has created a four-year program of problem-based mathematics that replaces the traditional Algebra I–Geometry–Algebra II/Trigonometry–Precalculus sequence and that is designed to exemplify the curriculum reform called for in the *Curriculum and Evaluation Standards* of the National Council of Teachers of Mathematics.

The IMP curriculum integrates traditional material with additional topics recommended by the NCTM *Standards*, such as statistics, probability, curve fitting, and matrix algebra. Although every IMP unit has a specific mathematical focus (for instance, similar triangles), most units are structured around a central problem and bring in other topics as needed to solve that problem, rather than narrowly restricting the mathematical content. Ideas that are developed in one unit are generally revisited and deepened in one or more later units.

For which students is the IMP curriculum intended?

The IMP curriculum is for all students. One of IMP's goals is to make the learning of a core mathematics curriculum accessible to everyone. Toward that end, we have designed the program for use with heterogeneous classes. We provide you with a varied collection of supplemental problems to give you the flexibility to meet individual student needs.

Teacher Phyllis Quick confers with a group of students.

How is the IMP classroom different?

When you use the IMP curriculum, your role changes from "imparter of knowledge" to observer and facilitator. You ask challenging questions. You do not give all the answers but you prod students to do their own thinking, to make generalizations, and to go beyond the immediate problem by asking themselves "What if?"

The IMP curriculum gives students many opportunities to write about their mathematical thinking, to reflect on what they have done, and to make oral presentations to each other about their work. In IMP, your assessment of students becomes integrated with learning, and you evaluate students in a variety of ways, including class participation, daily homework assignments, Problems of the Week, portfolios, and unit assessments. The IMP *Teaching Handbook* provides many practical suggestions for teachers on how to get the best possible results using this curriculum in *your* classroom.

What is in Year 1 of the IMP curriculum?

Year 1 of the IMP curriculum contains five units.

Patterns

The primary purpose of this unit is to introduce students to ways of working on and thinking about mathematics that may be new to them. In a sense, the unit is an overall introduction to the IMP curriculum, which involves changes for many students in how they learn mathematics and what they think of as mathematics. The main mathematical ideas of the unit include function tables, the use of variables, positive and negative numbers, and some basic geometrical concepts.

The Game of Pig

A dice game called Pig forms the core of this unit. Playing and analyzing Pig involves students in a wide variety of mathematical activities. The basic problem for students is to find an optimum strategy for playing the game. In order to find a good strategy and prove that it is optimum, students work with the concept of expected value and develop a mathematical analysis for the game based on an area model for probability.

The Overland Trail

This unit looks at the mid-nineteenth century western migration across what is now the United States in terms of the many mathematical relationships involved. These relationships involve planning what to take on the 2400-mile trek, estimating the cost of the move, studying rates of consumption and of travel, and estimating the time to reach the final goal. A major mathematical focus of the unit is the use of equations, tables, and graphs to describe real-life situations.

The Pit and the Pendulum

In Edgar Allan Poe's story, *The Pit and the Pendulum,* a prisoner is tied down while a pendulum with a sharp blade slowly descends. If the prisoner does not act, he will be killed by the pendulum. Students read an excerpt from the story, and are presented with the problem of whether the prisoner would have enough time to escape. To resolve this question, they construct pendulums and conduct experiments. In the process, they are introduced to the concepts of normal distribution and standard deviation as tools for determining whether a change in one variable really does affect another. They use graphing calculators to learn about quadratic equations and to explore curve fitting. Finally, after deriving a theoretical answer to the pendulum problem, students actually build a thirty-foot pendulum to test their theory.

Shadows

The central question of this unit is, "How can you predict the length of a shadow?" The unit moves quickly from this concrete problem to the geometric concept of similarity. Students work with a variety of approaches to come to an understanding of similar polygons, especially similar triangles. Then they return to the problem of the shadow, applying their knowledge of similar triangles and using informal methods for solving proportions, to develop a general formula. In the last part of the unit, students learn about the three primary trigonometric functions—sine, cosine, and tangent—as they apply to acute angles, and they apply these functions to problems of finding heights and distances.

How do the four years of the IMP curriculum fit together?

The four years of the IMP curriculum form an integrated sequence through which students can learn the mathematics they will need, both for further education and on the job. Although the organization of the IMP curriculum is very different from the traditional Algebra I–Geometry–Algebra II/Trigonometry–Precalculus sequence, the important mathematical ideas are all there.

Here are some examples of how both traditional concepts and topics new to the high school curriculum are developed.

Linear equations

In Year 1 of the IMP curriculum, students develop an intuitive foundation about algebraic thinking, including the use of variables, which they build on throughout the program. In the Year 2 unit *Solve It!,* students use the concept of equivalent equations to see how to solve any linear equation in a single variable. Later in Year 2, in a unit called *Cookies* (about maximizing profits for a bakery), they solve pairs of linear equations in two variables, using both algebraic and geometric methods. In the Year 3 unit *Meadows or Malls?,* they extend those ideas to systems with more than two variables, and see how to use matrices and the technology of graphing calculators to solve such systems.

Measurement and the Pythagorean theorem

Measurement, including area and volume, is one of the fundamental topics in geometry. The Pythagorean theorem is one of the most important geometric principles ever discovered. In the Year 2 unit *Do Bees Build It Best?,* students combine these ideas with their knowledge of similarity (from the Year 1 unit *Shadows*) to see why the hexagonal prism of the bees' honeycomb design is the most efficient regular prism possible. Students also use the Pythagorean theorem in later units, applying it to develop principles like the distance formula in coordinate geometry.

Trigonometric functions

In traditional programs, the trigonometric functions are introduced in the eleventh or twelfth grade. In the IMP curriculum, students begin working with trigonometry in Year 1 (in *Shadows*), using right-triangle trigonometry in several units (including *Do Bees Build It Best?*) in Years 2 and 3. In the Year 4 unit *High Dive,* they extend trigonometry from right triangles to circular functions, in the context of a circus act in which a performer falls from a Ferris wheel into a moving tub of water. (In *High Dive,* students also learn principles of physics, developing laws for falling objects and finding the vertical and horizontal components of velocity.)

Standard deviation and the binomial distribution

Standard deviation and the binomial distribution are major tools in the study of probability and statistics. *The Game of Pig* gets students started by building a firm understanding of concepts of probability and the phenomenon of experimental variation. Later in Year 1 (in *The Pit and the Pendulum*), they use standard deviation to see that the period of a pendulum is determined primarily by its length. In Year 2, they compare standard deviation with the chi-square test in examining whether a set of data is statistically significant. In *Pennant Fever* (Year 3), students use the binomial distribution to evaluate a team's chances of winning the baseball championship, and in *The Pollster's Dilemma* (Year 4), students tie many of these ideas together in the central limit theorem, seeing how the margin of error and the level of certainty for an election poll depend on its size.

Does the program work?

The IMP curriculum has been thoroughly field-tested by hundreds of classroom teachers around the country. Their enthusiasm comes from the success they have seen in their own classrooms with their own students. For those who measure success by test scores, we mention that repeated studies have proved that IMP students do at least as well as students in traditional mathematics classes on tests like the SAT, even though IMP students spend far less time than traditional students on the algebra and geometry skills emphasized by these tests. With the time saved, IMP students learn topics such as statistics that other students don't see until they reach college.

But one of our proudest achievements is that IMP students are excited about mathematics, as shown by the fact that they take more mathematics courses in high school than their counterparts in traditional programs. We think this is because they see that mathematics can be relevant to their own lives. If so, then the program works.

Dan Fendel
Diane Resek
Lynne Alper
Sherry Fraser

Note to Students

These pages in the student book welcome students to the program.

You are about to begin an adventure in mathematics, an adventure organized around interesting, complex problems. The concepts you learn grow out of what is needed to solve those problems.

This curriculum was developed by the Interactive Mathematics Program (IMP), a collaboration of teachers, teacher-educators, and mathematicians who have been working together since 1989 to reform the way high school mathematics is taught. About one hundred thousand students and five hundred teachers used these materials before they were published. Their experiences, reactions, and ideas have been incorporated into the final version you now hold.

Our goal is to give you the mathematics you need to succeed in this changing world. We want to present mathematics to you in a manner that reflects how mathematics is used and reflects the different ways people work and learn together. Through this perspective on mathematics, you will be prepared both for continued study of mathematics in college and for the world of work.

This book contains the various assignments that will be your work during Year 1 of the program. As you will see, these assignments incorporate ideas from many branches of mathematics, including algebra, geometry, probability, graphing, statistics, and trigonometry. Other topics will come up in later parts of this four-year program. Rather than present each of these areas separately, we have integrated them and presented them in meaningful contexts so that you'll see how they relate to one another and to our world.

Each unit in this four-year program has a central problem or theme, and focuses on several major mathematical ideas. Within each unit, the material is organized for teaching purposes into "Days," with a homework assignment for each day. (Your class may not follow this schedule exactly, especially if it doesn't meet every day.)

At the end of the main material for each unit, you will find a set of "supplemental problems." These problems provide additional opportunities for you to work with ideas from the unit, either to strengthen your understanding of the core material or to explore new ideas related to the unit.

Although the IMP program is not organized into courses called Algebra, Geometry, and so on, you will be learning all the essential mathematical concepts that are part of those traditional courses. You will also be learning concepts from branches of mathematics—especially statistics and probability—that are not part of a traditional high school program.

To accomplish this goal, you will have to be an active learner. Simply reading this book will not allow you to achieve your goal, because the book does not teach directly. Your role as a mathematics student will be to experiment, investigate, ask questions, make and test conjectures, and reflect, and then communicate your ideas and conclusions both verbally and in writing. You will do some work in collaboration with your fellow students, just as users of mathematics in the real world often work in teams. At other times, you will be working on your own.

We hope you will enjoy the challenge of this new way of learning mathematics and will see mathematics in a new light.

Dan Fendel   Diane Resek   Lynne Alper   Sherry Fraser

Finding What You Need

We designed this guide to help you find what you need amid all the information it provides. Each of the following components has a special treatment in the layout of the guide.

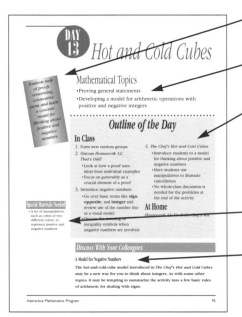

Synopsis of the Day: The key idea or activity for each day is summarized in a brief sentence or two.

Mathematical Topics: Mathematical issues for the day are presented in a bulleted list.

Outline of the Day: Under the *In Class* heading, the outline summarizes the activities for the day, which are keyed to numbered headings in the discussion. Daily homework assignments and Problems of the Week are listed under the *At Home* heading.

Special Materials Needed: Special items needed in the classroom for each day are bulleted here.

Discuss With Your Colleagues: This section highlights topics that you may want to discuss with your peers.

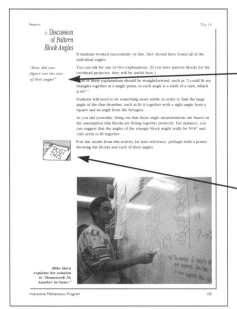

Suggested Questions: These are specific questions that you might ask during an activity or discussion to promote student insight or to determine whether students understand an idea. The appropriateness of these questions generally depends on what students have already developed or presented on their own.

Post This: The *Post This* icon indicates items that you may want to display in the classroom.

Icons for Student Written Products

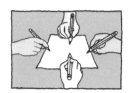

Single Group report

Individual reports

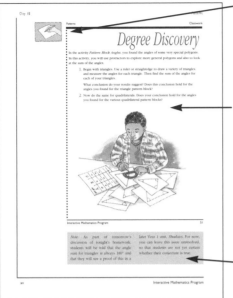

Icons for Student Written Products: For each group activity, there is an icon suggesting a single group report, individual reports, or no report at all. If graphs are included, the icon indicates this as well. (The graph icons do not appear in every unit.)

Embedded Student Pages: Embedded within the pages of the teacher guide are reduced-size copies of the pages from the student book. These reduced student pages include the "transition pages" that appear occasionally within each unit to summarize each portion of the unit and to prepare students for what is coming. Having all of these student pages in the teacher guide is a helpful way for you to see things from the students' perspective.

Asides: These are ideas outside the main thrust of a discussion. They include background information for teachers, refinements or subtle points that may only be of interest to some students, ways to help fill in gaps in understanding the main ideas, and suggestions about when to bring in a particular concept.

Additional Information

Here is a brief outline of other tools we have included to assist you and make both the teaching and the learning experience more rewarding.

Glossary: This section, which is found at the back of the book, gives the definitions of important terms for all of Year 1 for easy reference. The same glossary appears in the student book.

Appendix A: Supplemental Problems: This appendix contains a variety of interesting additional activities for the unit, for teachers who would like to supplement material found in the regular classroom problems. These additional activities are of two types—*reinforcements,* which help increase student understanding of concepts that are central to the unit, and *extensions,* which allow students to explore ideas beyond the basic unit.

Appendix B: Blackline Masters: For each unit, this appendix contains materials you can reproduce that are not available in the student book and that will be helpful to teacher and student alike. They include the end-of-unit assessments as well as such items as diagrams from which you can make transparencies. Semester assessments for Year 1 are included in *The Overland Trail* (for first semester) and *Shadows* (for second semester).

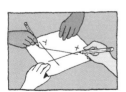

Single group graph

Individual graphs

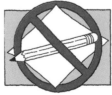

No report at all

Year 1 IMP Units

Patterns

The Game of Pig

The Overland Trail

The Pit and the Pendulum

Shadows   (in this book)

Contents

"Shadows" Overview

Summary of the Unit

This unit opens with the question, "How can you predict the length of a shadow?" Students do some initial, open-ended experiments to develop their curiosity and their intuitive feeling for how shadows work.

The general problem is refined to more specific ones, in which the length of a shadow is dependent on particular variables. Two general cases are introduced: "sun shadows," in which the shadow is cast by the sun or other object that is, for practical purposes, infinitely far away; and "lamp shadows," in which the shadow is cast by a street lamp or other "finite" light source.

Students are told that they will focus primarily on lamp shadows, and they then do further experiments in which they choose a single variable and gather data relating the length of the shadow to that variable, while leaving all other variables constant. They then look for an equation or formula to describe their data.

They will generally find that they cannot do so. (Their degree of success depends on which variable they are changing.) They are told that in order to understand how shadow lengths work, they need to learn some geometry.

Students begin their study of geometry by working with the intuitive idea of *same shape* to develop criteria for defining **similarity** for polygons. After some investigation and development of their own ideas, they are given the formal definition:

Two polygons are **similar** if

- their corresponding angles are equal, and

- their corresponding sides are proportional in length

By finding counterexamples, students see that, for polygons in general, meeting just one of these two conditions does not guarantee similarity. But they also discover that triangles are special: if two triangles have either corresponding angles equal or corresponding sides in proportion, they must be similar. Activities with concrete materials help give students an intuitive sense of why this is so.

The unit includes other work on criteria for similarity, including ideas about the use of parallel lines to establish equal angles. As another part of their work with similar triangles, students set up proportions, which they solve using informal methods. (Methods for solving equations based on equivalent expressions and equivalent equations are introduced in Year 2 of the Interactive Mathematics Program, after students have developed some confidence in their own informal methods.)

Students then apply their new knowledge of similar triangles to measuring heights of objects in several ways. One way involves the use of mirrors and the principle that the angle of incidence equals the angle of reflection. Students work with mirrors and flashlights to discover this principle.

In particular, students return to the lamp shadow problem, applying their knowledge of similar triangles and developing a formula for the length of this type of shadow in terms of the variables studied earlier.

In the last part of the unit, students learn about the three fundamental trigonometric functions—sine, cosine, and tangent—as defined in terms of right triangles. They apply these functions to problems in which heights and distances must be found and finally solve the sun shadow problem.

The overall organization of the unit and its primary activities can be summarized in the following schedule:

- Days 1–3: Introduction of the unit problem

- Days 4–6: Experiments on how shadow lengths vary and attempts to find functions to describe the results

- Days 7–13: Development of the concept of similarity and of the criteria for similarity; working with similar triangles, right triangles, and proportions

- Days 14–16: Principles about equal angles, including work with parallel lines

- Days 17–19: Application of similar triangles to indirect measurement problems

- Days 20–21: Solving the lamp shadow problem

- Days 22–25: Introduction of the trigonometric functions and solution of the sun shadow problem

- Days 26–28: Portfolios, end-of-unit assessments, and summing up

Concepts and Skills

The concept of similarity is the central theme of this unit. Through this concept, students explore a variety of ideas from geometry and algebra.

The main concepts and skills that students will encounter and practice during the course of this unit can be summarized by category as shown below.

Similarity and congruence

- Developing intuitive ideas about the meaning of "same shape" and learning the formal definitions of similarity and congruence

- Discovering criteria for polygons to be similar and, in particular, for triangles to be similar

- Working with the concept of corresponding parts of similar figures

- Applying properties of similar triangles to physical situations

- Using scale drawings to solve problems

The triangle inequality

- Discovering the triangle inequality

- Investigating the extension of the triangle inequality to polygons

Right triangles and trigonometry

- Learning standard terminology applied to right triangles, including *hypotenuse, leg, opposite,* and *adjacent*

- Learning the right triangle definitions of sine, cosine, and tangent

- Using sine, cosine, and tangent to solve problems

- Developing formulas relating sine and cosine

Algebra of proportions

- Developing equations of proportionality from situations involving similar figures

- Developing informal procedures for solving proportions

Logical reasoning and proof

- Working with the concept of *counterexample* in understanding the criteria for similarity

- Formulating and refining conjectures

- Proving that vertical angles are equal

- Proving the angle sum property for triangles using the properties of parallel lines

Parallel lines and angles

- Rediscovering the angle sum properties of polygons

- Discovering that vertical angles are equal

- Discovering the properties of angles formed by a transversal across parallel lines

Experiments and data

- Planning and carrying out controlled experiments

- Collecting and analyzing data

Other concepts and skills are developed in connection with Problems of the Week.

Materials

You will need to provide the following materials during this unit (in addition to standard materials such as graphing calculators, transparencies, chart paper, grid paper, marking pens, and so forth).

- Flashlights—one per group

- Wooden or plastic cubes—between 5 and 10 per group

- Metersticks or yardsticks—one per group

- Grid paper overhead transparencies (for presentations of *POW 16: Spiralaterals*)

- Straws—about 10 per group

- Dental floss (preferably unwaxed) or string—several feet per group

- Scissors—one per group

- Pipe cleaners (sometimes called chenille sticks at crafts stores)

- (Optional) A classroom demonstration protractor

- Mirrors (any size)—one per group or per pair (mirrored plexiglass is just as good)

Note: Students are supposed to provide their own rulers and protractors, but you may want to have a supply of these on hand in case students don't have them. They will be needed frequently throughout the unit.

Grading

The IMP *Teaching Handbook* contains general guidelines about how to grade students in an IMP class. You will probably want to check daily that students have done their homework, and include the regular completion of homework as part of students' grades. Your grading scheme will probably also include Problems of the Week, the unit portfolio, and end-of-unit assessments.

Because you will not be able to read thoroughly every assignment that students turn in, you will need to select certain assignments to read carefully and to base grades on. Here are some suggestions.

- Group reports on *Shadow Data Gathering* and *Looking for Equations* (Days 4-6)

- *Homework 12: Very Special Triangles*

- *More About Angles* (Day 15)

- *Homework 18: Mirror Madness*

- *A Shadow of a Doubt* (Day 20)

If you want to base your grading on more tasks, there are many other homework assignments, class activities, and oral presentations you can use.

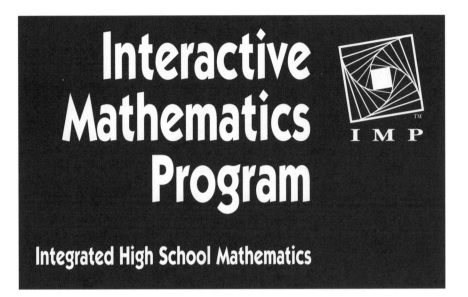

Interactive Mathematics Program

IMP

Integrated High School Mathematics

Y E A R 1

Shadows

Shadows

**Days
1–5**

What is a Shadow?

**This page in the
student book
introduces Days 1
through 5**

This unit asks the question, "How long is a shadow?" But
before you can answer this question, you need to think about
some others, such as, "What is a shadow?" "Where do

shadows come from?" and "Are
there different kinds of
shadows?"

If you see some resemblance
to *The Pit and the Pendulum*
in the early days of this unit,
don't be surprised. But
Shadows has its own set of
mathematical ideas for you to
learn, and the two units are
really quite different.

*Cody Boling, Ethan Fitzhenry, and
Nikki Robinson measure the length
of the shadow in the "Shadow Data
Gathering" experiment.*

Shadows and Spiralaterals

Students are introduced to the unit problem and begin work on POW 16.

Mathematical Topics

- General introduction to the unit problem
- Introduction to spiralaterals

Outline of the Day

In Class

1. Form new random groups
2. *Shadows*—introduction of unit problem
   - Have students read the problem
   - Discuss generally what causes shadows
3. Introduce *POW 16: Spiralaterals*
   - Have students make some spiralaterals to get a sense of how they are created

At Home

Homework 1: Shadows and Spiralaterals

POW 16: Spiralaterals (due Day 8)

1. Form New Groups

At the beginning of the unit, put students into groups as described in the IMP *Teaching Handbook*. We recommend that new groups be formed on Day 14.

This is a good time to mention to students that they will need protractors throughout this unit. The first use of protractors is on Day 6, where their use is reviewed in preparation for *Homework 6: Draw the Same Shape*.

2. *Shadows*
(see facing page)

"What causes shadows?"

Let students read *Shadows,* the introductory activity for the unit. You may want to have a brief class discussion about what shadows are and how and why they occur, without getting into the issue of shadow length.

For example, students should see that shadows represent the contrast between an area that gets light and an area where the light is blocked off. You can have a student shine a flashlight at the wall and have another student interpose an object, so students see the outline of the object in shadow. The students can then move either the flashlight or the object to see how this moves the shadow.

This discussion should be limited to no more than about 10 minutes, so the rest of the class time can be spent on the new POW.

"Think about why, at night, shadows might get bigger as you walk toward them."

Point out to students that part of tonight's homework asks them to think about the line in the riddle that says, "If you come toward me, I might get bigger (especially at night)," as a way of bringing out the two main types of shadows. (The other part of the homework is about the new POW.)

Tell students that tomorrow they will begin the unit problem in earnest with the activity *How Long Is a Shadow?*

3. Introduce POW 16: Spiralaterals
(see page 7)

After the brief introduction to the main unit problem, have the class look at *POW 16: Spiralaterals.*

Since this is such an open-ended investigation, you should take some class time to illustrate how a spiralateral is made, because seeing an example will be much clearer than reading a written description.

Then let students work together in groups on the problem, perhaps starting on Part II of tonight's homework.

Students should have grid paper of some kind for work on this assignment.

Discussion of this POW is scheduled for Day 8.

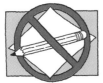

Shadows

A Riddle

As you walk around, I stay with you.

I'm sometimes ahead of you and sometimes behind you.

If you were smaller, I would be too.

If you come toward me, I often get bigger (especially at night).

If you shine a light on me, I disappear.

What am I?

Since the title of this unit is *Shadows,* you probably were able to guess the answer to this simple riddle.

Continued on next page

398

Interactive Mathematics Program

The Real Riddle

But there are some riddles about shadows that are not so clear. The big riddle for the unit is this:

> *How long is a shadow?*

It's easy to answer by saying, "It depends," but what does it depend on? You might consider these comparisons with previous work:

- In *The Pit and the Pendulum*, you saw that the period of a swinging pendulum is primarily determined by the pendulum's length. What variable or variables determine the length of a shadow?

- In *The Pit and the Pendulum*, you developed a formula based on experiments that estimated the period as a function of the pendulum's length. What kind of formula can you develop for the length of a shadow? And how should it be developed? Is there a better way than experimentation?

Your central task in this unit is to develop answers to these and similar questions.

POW 16   *Spiralaterals*

This POW is about spiralaterals. A spiralateral is a sequence of line segments that forms a spiral-like shape. It is easiest to draw spiralaterals if you use grid paper.

Each spiralateral is based on a sequence of numbers. To give an example, let's suppose your sequence is 3, 2, 4. To draw the spiralateral, you need to choose a starting point. The starting direction is always "up" on the paper.

The first number is 3, so the spiralateral begins with a segment that goes up 3 spaces, as in diagram A.

Before each new number, the spiralateral turns clockwise 90° (that is, a quarter turn to the right). So the second segment of the spiralateral will go to the right. The second number is 2, so the spiralateral moves 2 spaces in that direction. This gives diagram B.

Next, the spiralateral again turns clockwise 90° (so it's now facing "down"), and this time goes 4 spaces (because the third number in the sequence is 4), giving diagram C.

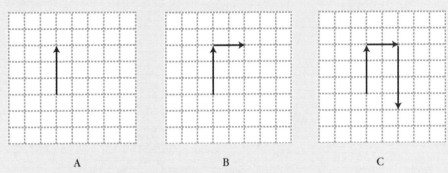

               A   B   C

You've now gotten to the end of the original three-number sequence.

But this is where it gets interesting. Instead of stopping, you go back to the beginning of the sequence and continue where you left off.

That is, make another 90° clockwise turn (so you're now going to the left), and move 3 spaces. And then another 90° turn and 2 up, a 90° turn and 4 right, a 90° turn and 3 down, and so on. Continue until you get back to the place where you started (if you ever do!). In other words, it's as if your sequence, instead of just being 3, 2, 4, was 3, 2, 4, 3, 2, 4, 3, 2, 4, 3, 2, 4, . . . , and so on, as long as necessary.

Continued on next page

In our example, the diagram will look like this after ten steps:

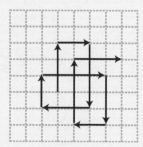

As you can see, in two more steps, you'll be back to the start. So the complete spiralateral for this sequence looks like this:

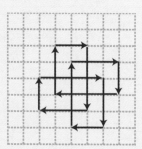

Your assignment for this POW is to explore the idea of spiralaterals. Here are some things you can do as part of your exploration.

• Make some spiralaterals, using your own sequences of numbers.

• Look for patterns.

• Make up questions about spiralaterals.

• Try sequences of different lengths.

• Make up new rules.

Whenever you come to a conclusion about spiralaterals, try to explain why your conclusion is true.

Reminder: Save your notes as you work on the problem. You will need them to do your write-up.

Continued on next page

Write-up

1. *Problem statement:* Explain what a spiralateral is and how it is formed.

2. *Process*

3. *Results and conclusions*:

   a. Show the results of some of the specific examples that you investigated, including diagrams as appropriate.

   b. What patterns did you notice among your results in part a? Summarize what you concluded from your examples, stating your conclusions clearly.

   c. Justify your conclusions as fully as you can. In other words, for any patterns that you found in your examples, explain why you believe that those patterns hold in general.

   d. What questions occurred to you as you worked on this problem that you did not discuss yet?

4. *Evaluation*

Homework 1

Shadows and Spiralaterals

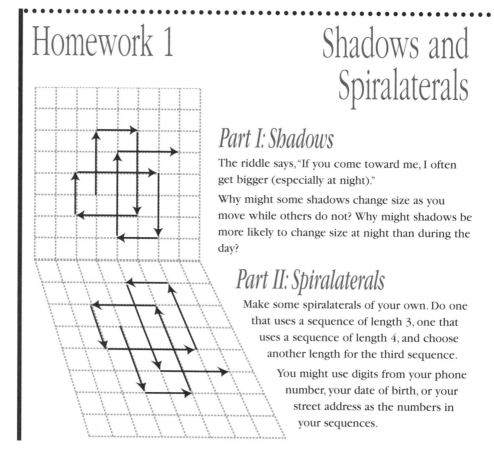

Part I: Shadows

The riddle says, "If you come toward me, I often get bigger (especially at night)."

Why might some shadows change size as you move while others do not? Why might shadows be more likely to change size at night than during the day?

Part II: Spiralaterals

Make some spiralaterals of your own. Do one that uses a sequence of length 3, one that uses a sequence of length 4, and choose another length for the third sequence.

You might use digits from your phone number, your date of birth, or your street address as the numbers in your sequences.

---

*Homework 1:
Shadows and
Spiralaterals*

This assignment gets students started both in thinking about the main unit problem and in working on their POW.

How Long Is a Shadow?

Mathematical Topics

- Brainstorming to identify factors that influence the length of a shadow
- Planning an experiment

Outline of the Day

In Class

1. Discuss Part II of *Homework 1: Shadows and Spiralaterals*
   - Check that students understand how to make spiralaterals
   - Bring out that not all spiralaterals return to their starting point
   - Part I to be discussed on Day 3

2. *How Long Is a Shadow?*
   - Groups brainstorm to identify variables that might affect the length of a shadow
   - Class compiles and posts list of variables

   - Groups design an experiment to be done at home to investigate how some variable affects shadow length

3. Discuss *How Long Is a Shadow?*
   - Be sure students are prepared for the experiments they will do for homework

At Home

Homework 2: Experimenting with Shadows

1. Discussion of *Homework 1: Shadows and Spiralaterals*

• *Part I: Shadows*

It is best to postpone discussion of the issues raised in Part I of the homework until after students have done some experiments. The discussion is scheduled to take place after tomorrow's discussion of tonight's homework.

• *Part II: Spiralaterals*

"Were you able to make some spiralaterals? Did they always come back to the starting place?"

Take just a few minutes to make sure students understood how to make spiralaterals, and have them share one or two observations. One observation that should come out is that, at least some of the time, spiralaterals based on a sequence of length 4 do not come back to their start.

You can suggest that the issue of which spiralaterals return and which do not is a good one to investigate, but don't attempt to resolve that question now.

2. *How Long Is a Shadow?*
(see page 14)

Today's activity has two parts. In the first part, students should come up with a list of variables that they think might influence the length of a shadow. After some initial discussion in their groups, the class will share ideas together. In the second part of the activity, each group will plan an experiment to test the influence of one of the variables. Students will individually carry out those experiments for homework.

This may be somewhat repetitive of the introductory discussion yesterday. If so, you can use this as an opportunity to get students to be more precise in identifying what they are measuring.

• *Part I: Defining Variables*

Have students work in groups for about 10 minutes on *Part I: Defining Variables.* Emphasize that they should make a written list and be as specific as possible, particularly in describing measurements.

"What variables did you consider?"

Then bring the class together as a whole to compile a master list of potential variables. As items get added to the list, be sure that they are clearly stated.

Save the list of variables for tomorrow. We suggest that you make this list on chart paper so that more detailed descriptions of these variables can be added tomorrow.

You may want to have each group turn in its own list of variables for Part I.

> *Note:* This is not the time to discuss whether or not a variable is "correct," that is, whether or not it really affects shadow length. Evaluation and selection of variables for further study will be done tomorrow.

• *Part II: Preparation for Homework 2: Experimenting with Shadows*

After compiling a master list, have students return to working in their groups. They should quickly select a variable to work with and begin Part II of the activity—planning their experiment. Tell them that their homework will be to carry out and write up the results of this experiment.

Emphasize that they can set up the experiment using whatever kind of shadow they want. For example, they can use the sun, a streetlight, or a flashlight as the light source; and they can use a building, a person, or a tree as the object. It is important that they try several different numerical values for the variable they are studying.

You may want to suggest that they work in pairs on the homework assignment in carrying out the experiment.

> The purpose of these experiments is to give students a general sense of the problem, not for students to obtain reliable data for analysis. They will do more careful experiments in class on Day 4 (in the activity *Shadow Data Gathering*).

3. Discussion of *How Long Is a Shadow?*

Bring the class together and have a few spade card students share their group's plan for tonight's experiments.

The purpose of this discussion is to ensure that students have some sort of plan when they leave today.

How Long Is a Shadow?

When you stand between a source of light and another object, your body blocks part of the light and casts a shadow on that other object.

For example, if you stand near a street lamp, as illustrated in the diagram above, your body casts a shadow on the ground.

The length of this shadow may depend on various **parameters** or **variables**, that is, on characteristics of the situation that can change from one example to another.

The central problem of the unit is to find out what variables the shadow length depends on and how the shadow length is determined by the values of those variables.

Part I: Defining Variables

Think of as many variables as possible that could affect the length of a shadow. (You may already have some ideas about this.)

Make a *written list* of these variables. Be very specific in describing your variables. For example, if you think a certain distance might be important, state exactly what that distance measures—*from* where *to* where.

When you have compiled a list, you can begin thinking about Part II.

Continued on next page

Part II: Preparation for "Homework 2: Experimenting with Shadows"

As a group, choose *one* of the variables that can be measured and write a careful plan for a set of experiments concerning this variable. The purpose of the experiments is to explore whether your variable really affects the length of a shadow and, if so, how changing the value of the variable affects shadow length.

Each person should make a copy of the plan your group creates. You will use this plan in doing the homework and will need to attach it to your write-up of the homework assignment.

Here are some ideas to keep in mind as the group puts the plan together.

- You should change only the variable that you are working with, keeping everything else constant. Your plan should state which variables you are keeping constant as well as the one you are changing.

- Think about the materials you might use in your experiment. For example, what will be your light source? What kind of object will cast the shadow? Include that information in your plan.

- Think about how you will change the value of the variable you are studying. You should try at least three different numerical values for this variable.

● ●

Homework 2   Experimenting with Shadows

In *How Long Is a Shadow?* your group planned an experiment to investigate how a particular variable might affect the length of a shadow. Your homework assignment is to carry out this experiment.

1. As closely as you can, carry out that plan, recording the results. (You may need to change the plan once you actually try to carry it out.)

2. Describe the results of your experiment, giving all the numerical data you collected. Include a diagram of your experiment. Make note of the specific values you used for the fixed variables.

3. Write about what you learned concerning the effect the variable you studied had on the length of shadows. State your conclusions clearly. Use the data you collected as evidence for your conclusions.

Attach to this homework your copy of the plan set up by your group.

Homework 2: *Experimenting with Shadows*

This homework is a continuation of today's classwork. You may want to suggest that students work in pairs on this assignment.

Refining the Question

Mathematical Topics

- Making the unit problem more precise
- Developing a diagram as a mathematical model of the unit problem

Outline of the Day

In Class

1. Discuss *Homework 2: Experimenting with Shadows*
   - Have students share experiences within their groups and make their presentations to the class
   - Discuss the difficulties of shadow experiments

2. Discuss Part I of *Homework 1: Shadows and Spiralaterals*
   - Identify two types of shadow problems:
     - ✔ lamp shadows
     - ✔ sun shadows

- Develop and post a diagram to refine the lamp shadow problem to focus on these variables:
  - ✔ the height of the light source (L)
  - ✔ the distance along the ground from the object to the light source (D)
  - ✔ the height of the object (H)

3. Optional: Discuss alternate shadow problems

At Home

Homework 3: Poetical Science

1. Discussion of *Homework 2: Experimenting with Shadows*

You might give students about five minutes to discuss within their groups the results of their homework experiments and to formulate a summary statement. While they are doing this, you may be able to identify students with good diagrams and have them prepare transparencies for overhead display later.

"What conclusions did your group reach from its experiments?"

After this initial discussion within groups, have club card students from various groups present the groups' conclusions about their chosen variables.

At this point, it is reasonable to expect that students will focus on qualitative conclusions rather than on detailed quantitative findings. For example, they may say the taller the object, the longer the shadow, without giving a specific formula relating the shadow length to height.

In fact, their comments may be limited to indicating what factors they think affect the length of the shadow, because that type of consideration was the focus of their attention for a large portion of the last unit, *The Pit and the Pendulum.*

As these reports are given, you can record students' summary statements directly on the list of variables that was compiled yesterday on chart paper. If students have conjectures, record those on chart paper also, and label them "conjecture."

• *The importance of careful experiments*

Spend some time having students share concerns about the logistics of their experiments—materials used, difficulties with measurement, and so forth.

"What difficulties did you have in carrying out your experiments?"

Ask students especially to talk about the difficulties they had in carrying out their experiments. Let them know that tomorrow they will do more careful experiments, in which each group will again focus on a single variable. Their goal in those experiments will be to gather numerical data that they might use to develop an equation relating shadow length to that variable.

2. Discussion of Part I of *Homework 1: Shadows and Spiralaterals*

Now is a good time to go back to Part I of *Homework 1: Shadows and Spiralaterals*. Your discussion will probably depend on the kinds of experiments students did in last night's homework.

"Why might shadows be more likely to change size at night than during the day?"

One approach is to ask students why they think shadows might be more likely to change size at night than during the day. Use their responses and the earlier discussion of homework experiments to bring out the distinction between two types of shadows.

- Shadows caused by the sun (or moon), where the light source is, in practical terms, infinitely far away. These will be called **sun shadows**.

- Shadows caused by such things as a lamp, a flashlight, or a streetlight, where changes in distance from the light source will affect the length of the shadow. These will be called **lamp shadows**.

You can tell students that, for most of the unit, they will be investigating *lamp shadows,* and that they will return to the issue of *sun shadows* near the end of the unit, except for perhaps a brief discussion now.

• *Refining the lamp shadow problem*

"If you worked with lamp shadows, what sort of diagrams did you use to describe your experiment?"

In order to get a more complete understanding of the situation, students are going to have to focus on a more precise question about shadows. One way to begin this refinement process is by having them share some of their diagrams from *Homework 2: Experimenting with Shadows,* calling for ideas from groups that did lamp shadow experiments.

"What exactly did you measure?"

As they present their diagrams, have them identify and label clearly the measurements that they used. For example, the phrase "the distance from the light to the object" is ambiguous; a diagram will show more clearly what is meant.

Try to get students to focus their attention on the lengths that are labeled *L, D,* and *H* in the diagram on the next page. Since these lengths were probably mentioned in some way by students in their presentations, one part of your task will be to focus attention on these particular parameters from among others that they may have considered.

As much as possible, this diagram should be developed by students. For example, if you identified students during the homework discussion who had good diagrams, you can have them present their ideas now.

"If you were to reduce this situation to its simplest form, what would a diagram of your experiment look like?"

Another aspect of developing the diagram is the elimination of details that are mathematically extraneous. For example, you might suggest that students represent the light by a point and the ground by a straight line.

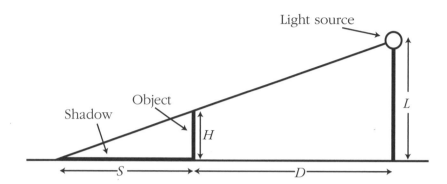

Once such a diagram has been developed, you should post it for reference for the duration of the unit.

As needed, help students to articulate verbal descriptions of these measurements. For example, they might offer these descriptions:

- L is the distance from the light source to the ground.

- D is the distance *along the ground* from the light source to the object casting the shadow.

- H is the height of the object casting the shadow.

Introduce the symbols L, D, and H as abbreviations for these measurements. Also introduce the symbol S for the length of the shadow itself (measured along the ground).

"How can you state the unit problem using these variables?"

This discussion, in which the problem is refined, can be summarized by the formulation of a goal for the unit.

You will probably want to post this goal.

> **Unit Goal: To find a formula expressing S, the length of the shadow, in terms of the variables L, D, and H.**

"How can you state the goal using 'f(x)' notation?"

Ask students if they can use the "$f(x)$" function notation introduced in *The Pit and the Pendulum* to express the type of formula they will be looking for. Help them as needed to develop a generic function equation, such as $S = f(L, D, H)$. You can explain that this notation is essentially a shorthand which suggests that there could be an In-Out table with three inputs (L, D, and H) and one output (S). In this notation, f represents the rule for the table.

You can include this formulation in the posted goal.

Keep in mind that function notation is fairly new to students and often difficult for them to use. Also, this is the first time that they are seeing function notation used with more than one independent variable. Therefore, you may need to do more leading than usual in order to get students to formulate this generic function equation.

Don't worry if some students are not comfortable with this formulation of the problem. They will be working with function notation throughout the four-year curriculum, and this exposure is one opportunity to get them used to it.

• *Articulating assumptions*

"What assumptions are you making by using this diagram?"

Using the diagram above involves some assumptions about the situation, and it may help to make these explicit. For example, the diagram assumes that

- the shadow is caused by a single light source
- the ground is level
- the object casting the shadow is vertical

Even with these assumptions stated, students may not believe that the three parameters, L, D, and H, actually determine the shadow length, S. One indirect goal of the unit is to enable them to see that, within the framework of these assumptions, S can be found in terms of the other variables.

You should post a list of these assumptions, perhaps leaving room for others to be added later on.

• *A mathematical model*

"What does 'mathematical model' mean?"

Tell students that this diagram represents a **mathematical model** for the shadow problem. Ask if they know what this means. The key idea to emphasize is that the term refers to the use of a mathematical or abstract description of a real-world situation.

You might mention that such models generally involve simplifications or assumptions like those just discussed, so any conclusions that are based on the model should be tested in the real situation if possible.

3. Optional: Alternate Shadow Problems

Although the main focus of the unit is on the lamp shadow problem, you may want to take some time here to talk about alternate shadow problems. You can use the following discussion for ideas.

You might mention to students that they will return to the sun shadow problem later in the unit. Make your own decision about whether to discuss the diagram for the sun shadow problem now or to wait until it comes up later.

• *More on sun shadows*

If the sun or another distant object were used as the light source, then the problem would change character, since L and D could not be treated as variables in the same way as was done for lamp shadows. If possible, get students to talk about the experience of walking along and seeing their shadow moving along with them without changing its length.

As will be discussed later in the unit (see Day 24), it makes more sense in the sun shadow problem to focus on the angle from the light source to the object (shown as θ below). That is, students will be looking for a function of the form $S = f(H, \theta)$.

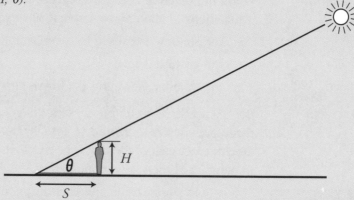

Note: You may need to introduce the Greek letter θ (*theta*) to students. You can tell them that it is commonly used in mathematics to represent angles.

• *Angle as variable*

Even in the lamp shadow situation, one could use the angle as one of the parameters that determines the length of the shadow. However, the angle is not independent of L, D, and H. That is, it is impossible to keep L, D, and H fixed and change the angle. However, if the idea of an angle as a variable comes up, you can acknowledge that one could use this as one of the basic parameters, and you can tell students that they will come back to look at this variable near the end of the unit when they examine the sun shadow problem.

• *Other types of shadows*

You may also want to acknowledge that there are some other variations to the shadow question besides the basic lamp shadow and sun shadow approaches.

For example, one might set up the situation so that the shadow is cast upon a wall instead of on the ground (perhaps using a light source on the ground). There is a supplemental problem, *Some Other Shadows,* suggesting ideas for students on such an investigation.

Homework 3   Poetical Science

Augusta Ada Byron (1815–1852) was the daughter of the famous English poet George Gordon Byron (usually known by his title as Lord Byron) and a mathematician, Anne Isabella Milbanke Byron. Augusta Ada Byron is known today as Ada Lovelace, having married Lord Lovelace.

At the time she lived, people thought there was a sharp separation between the kinds of skills needed for the sciences and the type of ability involved in creative arts like poetry.

This conflict between science and poetry was an ancient one, going back at least to the Greek philosopher Plato. He was suspicious of poetry and felt that "it gives no truth of its own, stirs up the emotions, and thereby blinds mankind to the real truth."

Ada Lovelace was unusual for her time, perhaps because of her parents' combination of interests. Her formal education was traditional in its emphasis on "the facts," but her father's imaginative influence kept appearing. Her teacher thought that studying mathematics would "cure" Ada of being too imaginative, but Ada responded that she had to use her imagination in order to understand mathematics.

Lovelace was herself a mathematics teacher and encouraged her students to use their imagination. She emphasized metaphors and visual images, and suggested that they use colored pens, rulers, and compasses (which were then considered "vulgar instruments") to make drawings that would help their understanding.

Continued on next page

Homework 3:
Poetical Science

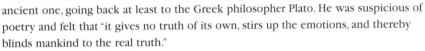

Tonight's homework is not directly tied to the unit. Instead, students read a brief biography that focuses on the nature of the scientific personality and suggests that certain stereotypes about scientific thinking may not be valid. Students are asked to think about how they use *imagination* in mathematics class.

• •

She wrote, "Imagination is the *Discovering* Faculty preeminently. It is that which penetrates into the unseen worlds around us, the worlds of Science. It is that which feels & discovers what *is*, the REAL which we see not, which *exists* not for our *senses*."

At the age of 18, she met Charles Babbage, who was then in the process of inventing what became the world's first computer. Working with him was the realization of a dream, because it allowed her to combine her imagination with her analytical skills. She was able to work on mathematics as a joy, not as the duty it had been when her mother made her study it.

Lovelace played an important role in the development of computer science by explaining Babbage's inventions to a larger audience. In her written *Notes*, she created a unified vision of their usefulness, combining metaphors about the creative power of the machines with detailed technical descriptions of their operation.

In honor of these contributions, a modern computer language has been named after her. The language Ada is one of the most sophisticated tools for studying artificial intelligence and is used by the military.

This article is adapted from the preface "Poetical Science" in the book *Ada, The Enchantress of Numbers* by Betty Alexandra Toole, Strawberry Press, Mill Valley, CA. The book contains Ada's letters and her description of the first computer.

Your Assignment

1. The article talks about the use of imagination in understanding mathematics. Think about two situations this year when your imagination helped you *in this class*. Write about those experiences.

2. Do you agree or disagree with what Plato said about poetry? Write what you think about poetry and truth.

Shadow Data Gathering

Students begin a 3-day segment, doing more shadow experiments.

Mathematical Topics

- Conducting controlled experiments

Outline of the Day

In Class

1. Discuss *Homework 3: Poetical Science*
   - Have students share ideas about the use of imagination
2. *Shadow Data Gathering*
   - Groups each focus on one of the key variables—*L, D,* or *H*
   - Emphasize keeping other parameters fixed

- The data will be posted on Day 5 and used in *Looking for Equations*

At Home

Homework 4: *An N-by-N Window*

Special Materials Needed

- 1 flashlight per group
- 5–10 cubes per group
- 1 meterstick or yardstick per group

Discuss With Your Colleagues

Why Do Experiments?

As this teacher's guide points out, the experiments and analysis that students do on Days 4 through 6 are largely fruitless in terms of concrete formulas. You and your colleagues may want to discuss how students (and you) react to this experience, working from the ideas in today's subsection, "Why do experiments?"

1. Discussion of *Homework 3: Poetical Science*

You can have several students each read about a time when they used their imagination in this class.

"Which occupations require a great deal of imagination?"

If the students seem interested, you might have a class discussion about which occupations require a great deal of imagination and why.

Use your judgment about whether or not to take time on Question 2.

2. *Shadow Data Gathering*
(see page 28)

The next three days, containing the activities *Shadow Data Gathering* and *Looking for Equations,* form a segment in which students tackle the shadow problem using an approach similar to that used in the last unit, *The Pit and the Pendulum.*

* *For teachers: An overview of experiments and the search for formulas on Days 4 through 6*

With the unit goal and refinement of the problem in mind, the groups will spend the balance of Day 4 and all of Days 5 and 6 approaching the lamp shadow problem experimentally. Each group will gather data relating the shadow length, S, to one of the other three variables—L, D, or H—and will make an In-Out table for their data. They will prepare their results from the activity *Shadow Data Gathering* as a chart-paper report to be posted for other groups to use.

They will then use various approaches to try to find equations that explain their data. They will also have the opportunity to study data gathered by other groups. They do this in the activity *Looking for Equations.*

After completing *Looking for Equations* on Day 6, each group should turn in a report summarizing its work for these three days of experiments and analysis. Their earlier chart-paper report (from *Shadow Data Gathering*) is part of this overall report.

For simplicity, the day-by-day guide has them doing the experiments on Day 4, examining their own data on Day 5, and examining other data and summarizing results on Day 6, but the activities do not need to fit this schedule precisely. The homework assigned on Days 4 and 5 does not require them to keep to this schedule.

* *Why do experiments?*

When students examine the results of their experiments (in the activity *Looking for Equations*), they will discover that, for at least two of the variables, there is no simple rule that they can get from their data explaining the information in the In-Out table.

The unit will then turn to a completely different approach to the problem, analyzing shadow length by developing certain geometric concepts, especially similarity, and applying those concepts to the basic lamp shadow diagram.

In effect, the experimental work here in the early part of the unit will not be used in solving the unit problem. So you may wonder why several days of the unit are devoted to this "unproductive" approach.

There are several reasons why we have chosen to start the unit this way.

- The experiments that students do at the beginning of the unit get them physically involved in the central problem.

- The desire to explain the experimental results and describe them algebraically provides part of the motivation

to students for the geometric analysis that is the mainstay of the unit.

- The experiments are helpful in convincing students that the three parameters under consideration—*L, D,* and *H*—are really important in determining shadow length.

- Although one can do the geometric analysis abstractly, many students will appreciate it more because of the more tactile sense of the problem that they develop through the experiments.

- The experimental approach creates a smooth follow-up to students' work in *The Pit and the Pendulum.* Coming out of their work in that unit, students are likely to see experimentation as a natural approach.

• *Introducing the activity*

You might let each group choose one of the three variables—*L, D,* or *H*—to experiment with, but be sure to have at least one group working with each of the three variables. (If possible, have at least two working with each variable.)

Distribute these materials for the experiments:

- Flashlights as the light source

- Cubes to build the object casting the shadow

- Metersticks or yardsticks for measuring distances

Note: It will be helpful to put tape over part of the flashlight's opening in order to focus the light more directly on the object casting the shadow. It will also help students if they can place their materials on grid paper that uses the same units as the

cubes, so they can mark their measurements directly on the grid paper.

Groups can complete *Shadow Data Gathering* tomorrow and can then immediately begin the activity *Looking for Equations,* in which they

Shadow Data Gathering

In *The Pit and the Pendulum*, you used experiments to find a relationship between the length of the pendulum and the pendulum's period.

The general approach in that unit was to gather data and then look for a function that fit the data.

In this activity and in *Looking for Equations,* you will be using the same approach for the shadow problem.

Continued on next page

try to analyze the relationship between their chosen variable and shadow length. This analysis will be completed and discussed on Day 6.

Remind students to record the fixed values that they use in their experiments, even though the activity tells them explicitly to do so. As they work, they may ask about the level of accuracy needed in their measurements. You can let them work out their own ideas for dealing with this issue.

You have seen that the length of a shadow seems to depend on three parameters or variables:

- The height of the light source (*L*)
- The distance from the object to the light source (*D*)
- The height of the object (*H*)

Using *S* for the length of the shadow, the central problem of the unit might be stated in this way:

> *What formula can be used to express S as a function of the variables L, D, and H? That is, how can you get a formula for a function f so that S = f(L, D, H)?*

Your Task

Your task in this assignment is to focus on just *one* of these three variables, keeping the other two fixed. For example, if your chosen variable is *H*, then you would pick specific values for *L* and *D*, and gather data about how *S* changes as you change *H*.

Your data should be organized into an In-Out table in which the input is your chosen variable and the output is the length of the shadow.

Your group will need to prepare a report on its work. The report should include your In-Out table, in a form appropriate for display.

The report should also include

- identification of your chosen variable
- a diagram of your experiment, which includes the *fixed values* used in your experiments for the other variables

For example, if *height of the light source* is your chosen variable, then you should keep the height of the object and the distance from the object to the light source fixed throughout the experiments. The values used for these other variables should be stated in your report and shown on your diagram.

Homework 4 An *N*-by-*N* Window

The central problem of this unit is to find a formula relating shadow length to certain other variables, either based on experiments or using some other method.

This problem also involves finding a formula, although the setting is completely different.

The diagram to the right shows the frame for a window 3 feet by 3 feet.

The frame is made of wood strips that separate the glass panes. Each glass pane is a square that is 1 foot wide and 1 foot tall.

As the numbering in the diagram shows, it would take 24 feet of wood strip to build a frame for a window 3 feet by 3 feet.

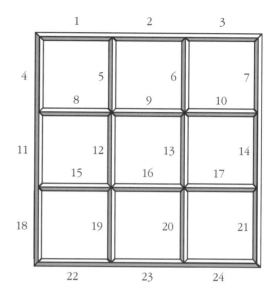

Your task is to develop a formula for the total length of wood strip needed to build square windows of different sizes.

You may want to do this by gathering data and making an In-Out table from different examples. Or you may prefer to study the window looking for insights that lead directly to a formula. (Or you may do a combination of both.)

In either case, generalize the problem to a window *N* feet by *N* feet. As usual, include all drawings, In-Out tables, and graphs.

Homework 4: An *N-by-N* Window

Tonight's homework involves finding a numerical formula to describe a situation. Students will probably use an In-Out table to organize their data, and then look for a pattern. This homework will also give them practice in working with variables.

Finding Formulas

Mathematical Topics

- Finding a formula to fit an In-Out table
- Looking for equations that fit experimental data

Outline of the Day

In Class

1. Discuss *Homework 4: An N-by-N Window*
   - Rules might be found either by inspection of the table or by analysis of the situation
   - Optional: Discussion of different rules for the same In-Out table
2. Post the data from *Shadow Data Gathering*
   - No discussion is needed; use the data for the next activity

3. *Looking for Equations*
   - Groups use different methods to look for rules for In-Out tables from *Shadow Data Gathering*
   - The activity will be discussed on Day 6

At Home

- *Homework 5: More About Windows*

Special Materials Needed

- 1 flashlight per group
- 5–10 cubes per group
- 1 meterstick or yardstick per group

1. Discussion of Homework 4: An N-by-N Window

"What formula did you come up with?"

You can have students share their formulas with each other in groups. Then let several diamond card students share their methods and results.

You may have some students use an approach of looking for patterns in the In-Out table while others use an approach based more on the geometry of the situation.

As suggested in the assignment, some students may compile an In-Out table like this one.

Length of side of window	Total length of wood needed
1	4
2	12
3	24
4	40

Students who create this sort of table may be able to figure out a rule based on the data. Others may create the table but not be able to find an algebraic expression that describes it.

Some students may take a different, more analytical, approach. For example, they may see that there will be $N + 1$ rows of horizontal wood strips, with N feet in each row, and an equal amount of vertical wood strips.

If both of these approaches come up, bring out their different nature, and tell students that they will have to see which approach works best for the shadow problem. You can also ask which approach is most similar to what they did in *The Pit and the Pendulum*.

You can point out that though their pendulum data showed a graph like a square root function, they had no reason based on the physics of the pendulum to believe that such a function would work. You can mention that an analytic approach based on principles of physics would show that a square root function should give a very good approximation, but wouldn't fit perfectly.

If students only use the In-Out table approach and find a rule, ask if they can see why that rule must work in all cases. This may lead them to the more analytic approach, which can be seen as a proof of the formula they found from the data.

• *Different rules for the same situation*

"Can both of these formulas be correct? What would that mean?"

You may have students who come up with different algebraic expressions that fit the data or describe the situation [for example, $2N(N + 1)$ and $N(2N + 2)$]. You can ask what it means to have two different formulas.

You can also suggest that they try to reconcile differing formulas, looking for reasons why different expressions give the same results.

Optional: If groups have trouble reconciling their formulas, you might suggest that they graph the formulas as functions on the graphing calculator and see if they produce the same graph. If the graphs are the same, then the rules are, in some sense at least, describing the same function. (Of course, this approach will only indicate that the portions of the graphs showing in the viewing rectangle are the same. Caution students about the fact that the graphs may be different elsewhere.)

Students will study the algebra of equivalent expressions in *Solve It!* in Year 2 of the IMP curriculum.

2. Posting Data from *Shadow Data Gathering*

Have each group post its results from *Shadow Data Gathering,* relating shadow length to its chosen variable. The posted report should include an In-Out table with the variable for the *In* identified clearly as *L, D,* or *H.*

The reports should also include the values students used for the variables they kept fixed and should be posted in the classroom.

3. *Looking for Equations*
(see page 35)

In *Looking for Equations,* each group is to look for an equation or formula that describes its In-Out table.

Because groups have only approximate data, there is a wide range of possible formulas that they might develop that come close to their data. However, you should be aware that only the groups using *D* as their chosen variable have a good chance to come up with a correct formula between shadow length and their variable, since the relationships between *S* and *L* and between *S* and *H* are too complex to be analyzed from the kind of data they will be getting.

The groups studying the relationship between *S* and *D* will probably discover that they can approximate the relationship by an equation of the form

$$S = cD$$

where *c* is a constant that depends on the fixed values being used for *L* and *H.* From the students' point of view, they should simply see data in which the value of *S* is a fixed number (called *c* in the equation above) times the value of *D,* and in which the graph of the data looks like a straight line. There is no reason to expect them to analyze the reason for the specific value they get for *c.* This number is just an experimental measurement to them.

The other groups are likely to feel some frustration, since they may be unable to come up with a formula that works well.

You should tell *all* groups, in a neutral way, that experimental data won't always fit into a nice formula, and that their task is just to do the best that they can.

If a group finds what it thinks is a good equation for its data, they should keep a record of it. Perhaps they can write it on a piece of paper and attach it, face down, to their posted report.

The group can then begin to look for a formula for another group's posted set of data. They should work with a set of data that studies each of the other variables before examining another set based on the variable that they used.

Each group will prepare a written report tomorrow describing their work for Days 4 through 6. Their poster report on *Shadow Data Gathering* should be included as the first part of this comprehensive report. The second part should contain their results on *Looking for Equations*—both for their own data and for the data of other groups.

Note: You may want to do some review of how to enter and plot on the graphing calculator. You could do this with a group that finishes gathering data early and then ask them to assist other groups.

Homework 5: More About Windows
(see page 36)

This assignment is a follow-up to last night's homework and asks students to generalize to arbitrary rectangular window frames.

Note: Students will need protractors for tomorrow night's homework. If you plan to review protractor use tomorrow, you may want to alert students to be sure to bring protractors to class.

Looking for Equations

You now have an In-Out table that shows data relating one of the shadow variables, *L, D,* or *H,* to the shadow length, *S.* Other groups have made similar tables.

Your next task is to analyze these In-Out tables, looking for equations connecting the *Out* values to the *In* values.

Start with your own In-Out table.

You might choose to look at the table directly, examining the pairs of numbers and looking for patterns. You can organize the entries in any way that makes sense to you. If you think it would be helpful to have additional pairs for your table, do the necessary experiments to find the appropriate information.

You might also try graphing your data, either by using pencil and paper or by entering the data in a graphing calculator. If you make a graph, choose scales for the axes that seem suitable to your data. Examine whether the points on your graph form a familiar shape.

When you find an equation that describes your data well, or if you decide that you are unable to find a reasonable rule to fit the data, you should move on to another group's set of data.

Homework 5   More About Windows

In *Homework 4: An N-by-N Window,* you investigated the length of wood strip needed for window frames like the one at the right.

In that assignment, your goal was to find a general formula for the amount of wood strip needed for a square window frame of any size.

Now, try to generalize to an arbitrary rectangular window frame. That is, get a formula in terms of M and N for the amount of wood strip needed for the frame of an M-by-N window.

As in *Homework 4: An N-by-N Window,* you may want to gather data about a variety of examples into an In-Out table and then look for a pattern in your data. If so, once you gather data, look for an algebraic rule that describes your table.

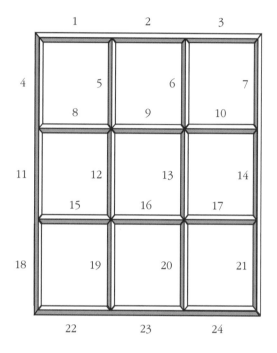

Or you may prefer a more analytic approach, in which you reason through why such a window frame should use a particular amount of wood strip. If you find a rule this way, verify it using some examples.

**Days
6–9**

The Geometry of Shadows

***This page in the
student book
introduces Days 6
through 9***

You've done some measurements involving shadows, and now it's time to try a different approach.

For a while, you're going to leave the world of shadows and enter the more abstract realm of geometry. Angles, polygons, lengths of sides—these will be the focus of your attention for much of the unit, but eventually these ideas will fit together to answer the shadowy questions that are lurking in the background.

*Jackie Hernandez shows
the class possible
counterexamples.*

414   Interactive Mathematics Program

Finding Formulas, Continued

Students share the results of their search for formulas and consider a different approach to the unit problem.

Mathematical Topics

- Finding a formula to fit an In-Out table
- Looking for a theoretical explanation for a formula
- Looking for equations that fit experimental data

Outline of the Day

In Class

1. Discuss *Homework 5: More About Windows*
2. Complete work on *Looking for Equations* (from Day 5)
3. Discuss *Looking for Equations*
   - Groups examining the variable *D* will probably see a linear relationship between *D* and *S*
   - Other groups will probably not be able to find a formula to fit their data
   - Use the lack of formulas as a motivation to study the geometry of the shadow problem
4. Discuss where to go next in trying to solve the unit problem
5. Review angle measurement, especially the angle of a polygon, in preparation for the homework

At Home

Homework 6: Draw the Same Shape

Special Materials Needed

- (Optional) A classroom demonstration protractor

1. Discussion of *Homework 5: More About Windows*

You can let volunteers share their ideas and approaches for the homework. As with *Homework 4: An N-by-N Window,* there are both *experimental* and *analytic* approaches.

Some students may have experimented with examples, made an In-Out table for their results (with two inputs for *M* and *N*), and then looked for a rule to describe the relationship between the *Out* (the amount of wood strip needed) and the two *Ins. Note:* The formula is not one that jumps out of the numbers easily, so students who just work from a table may not find a formula. There is no need to push for an algebraic rule for the problem.

Other students may have tried to analyze the geometry of the problem and developed a formula in that way.

Encourage students to use these two approaches to reinforce each other. For example, if a student develops a formula by analyzing the geometry, have the student test the formula with examples.

On the other hand, if a student initially gathers data from examples, and then finds a formula, urge the student to look for an explanation in the context of the problem.

2. Completing Work on *Looking for Equations*

Students should finish looking for formulas for their In-Out tables. Do not let a group get bogged down working on their own set of data. If they cannot find a formula that is satisfactory to them, tell them to leave it and work on a set of data involving a different one of the three variables, *L, D,* and *H.* If time allows, have each group work on at least one set of data for each variable.

As described in yesterday's notes, each group should prepare a written report describing its work for Days 4 through 6.

3. Discussion of *Looking for Equations*

"What formulas did your group find?"

Ask the heart card student in each group to report on the formulas the group found. If groups have different answers, discuss which, if any, are better answers.

As indicated in the Day 5 notes, if students gathered accurate data, they should see a linear relationship between S and D, which will have the form $S = cD$, where the constant c depends on the fixed values used for L and H.

Students should see that it is difficult to get formulas when the variable being studied is either L or H.

• *Shadows versus pendulums: The difficulty in having three variables that "matter"*

Students may feel frustrated that they were not successful in using their results to get the desired equations. They may see the shadow problem as analogous to their work on pendulums in the last unit, and they may think they should be able to get a formula based on experimental results.

"How is the shadow problem different from the pendulum problem?"

You might ask them to discuss how this situation is different from their work with pendulums.

As a hint, you might ask what variables they considered in *The Pit and the Pendulum* and which of them turned out to be important, and then ask similar questions about the shadow problem.

Help students see that, with shadows, they are dealing with three separate variables that affect the length of the shadow. Another important distinction is that in *The Pit and the Pendulum* they were interested in a specific situation (the 30-foot pendulum), while in this unit, the goal is to find a general formula.

4. Now What?

"So what should be done about the shadow problem?"

Ask students where this leaves them in terms of the central shadow problem. They should see that an approach based purely on gathering data is probably inadequate.

Tell them that in order to develop complete formulas relating S to L, D, and H, and to understand the relationships among these variables, they need to understand some geometry.

They will now spend several weeks studying geometrical concepts that may not seem directly related to shadows. Then they will return to thinking about shadows and connect the geometry to the unit problem.

5. Review of Angles

Be sure that students recall how to use a protractor. They also may need a review of angles: What is a 90° angle? What is a 135° angle? Review the fact that a complete turn is defined as 360°, and so 90° represents a quarter turn.

Some students may have difficulty with the idea of angle measurement for angles of a polygon, and some review of that may be needed as well.

For example, have students look at the diagram in Question 2 of tonight's *Homework 6: Draw the Same Shape,* focusing on the angle labeled 135° below.

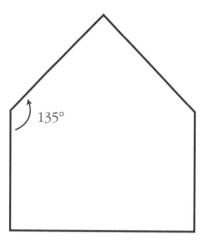

"What is the 'turn' involved in this angle?"

Point out that this angle is measured from the point of view of someone standing at the vertex, first looking along one side of the polygon and then turning to look along the other side.

Be sure students see that this is different from the angle through which you would turn if you were traveling along one side and then turned to continue along the other side.

For example, suppose you were moving up along the left side of the house and then, instead of continuing straight along the dotted line shown below, you turned along the roof. In making this change of direction, you would turn through a 45° angle.

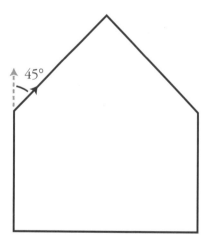

The 45° angle shown in the diagram above is called an **exterior angle** of the polygon. Exterior angles are discussed in the supplemental problem *Exterior Angles and Polygon Angle Sums.*

Homework 6   Draw the Same Shape

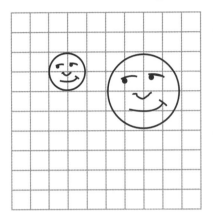

1. Draw a small, simple picture on a sheet of grid paper.

    Then draw another version of your picture that is *exactly the same shape* as the first one. Your second drawing should be *larger* than the original. (You have to decide what "exactly the same shape" means to you.)

2. Renata was making illustrations for a book on basic drawing technique. She came up with the figure below as the first step for drawing a house.

    Kim decided he liked this shape, but needed a bigger version of the house for his work.

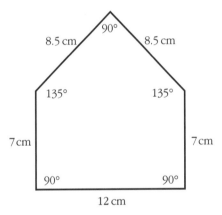

   a. Give a set of length and angle measurements that you think Kim might be able to use in place of those shown in the diagram above.

   b. Carefully draw a diagram that has your suggested measurements and compare it to Renata's. Does it have the same shape?

Continued on next page

Interactive Mathematics Program   415

Homework 6:
Draw the Same
Shape

Each student will need a piece of grid paper for Question 1 of the homework. Remind students that they need to have protractors and rulers for use at home. They may want them tonight.

3. Consider the following pairs of figures. In each case, state whether you consider them to be the same shape or not, and why.

a.

b.

c.

d.

4. Based on your experience with Questions 1 through 3, write your ideas in response to this question:

   How can you create a diagram that has exactly the same shape as a given one?

A House of the Same Shape

Mathematical Topics

- Identifying characteristics of figures having the same shape

Outline of the Day

In Class

1. Select presenters for tomorrow's discussion of *POW 16: Spiralaterals*

2. Discuss *Homework 6: Draw the Same Shape*
   - Leave the definition of "same shape" unresolved for now (the formal definition of similarity to be introduced on Day 8)

3. *How to Shrink It?*
   - Students examine different proposals for making a smaller version of a drawing

4. Discuss *How to Shrink It?*
   - Listen for student language that will help prepare the class for the formal definition of similarity

At Home

Homework 7: The Statue of Liberty's Nose

Special Materials Needed

- Grid paper transparencies (for tomorrow's POW presenters)

Discuss With Your Colleagues

Why Not Give Students the Definition Right Away?

The concept of similarity is the mathematical centerpiece of this unit, yet the formal definition doesn't come until Day 8. Prior to this, students do several activities, including *Homework 6: Draw the Same Shape* and *How to Shrink It?* (Day 7), in which they develop their own ideas about "same shape."

Discuss how these earlier activities pave the way for the formal definition, and how students' understanding of and attitude about that definition are affected by their own work in constructing their own concept.

1. POW Presentation Preparation

Presentations of *POW 16: Spiralaterals* are scheduled for tomorrow. Choose three students to make POW presentations, and give them overhead transparencies and pens to take home to use in their preparations. If possible, give them *grid paper* transparencies, that is, transparencies with grid lines.

2. Discussion of Homework 6: Draw the Same Shape

You do not need to discuss Question 1 of the homework. Students probably did a wide variety of different illustrations.

"What did you draw for Question 2?"

For Question 2, you can ask two or three students to draw their figures, showing the measurements for each side and angle, and let the class discuss whether their figures are the same shape as Renata's.

At present, you should leave the question unresolved. That is, tell students that, for now, they might disagree about what "same shape" means, but that they will be working toward the formal definition that mathematicians use.

Similarly, on Question 3, there will probably be some differences of opinion. Some students will say that "same shape" includes "facing the same way," so they will not consider the pair of rectangles in Question 3a or the pair of triangles in Question 3d to be the same shape.

On Question 3c, some students may consider these two triangles to be the same shape, even though the ratios of height to width are different, and some may even consider the pentagon and hexagon of Question 3b to be the same, even though the number of sides is different.

"Do you consider the mirror image of something to be the same shape?"

No absolute conclusions need to come out of this discussion, but help students to define what the issues are that they agree and disagree about. For example, you might post as questions to be resolved, "Is the mirror image of something considered the same shape?" or "Does changing the size of something change its shape?"

Keep alert for and highlight any comments that hint at the idea of ratio or proportion, since this is one of the foundations of the formal definition of similarity. For example, a student might say, concerning the triangles in Question 3c, "The triangle on the right is taller so it should also be wider, but it isn't, so it isn't the same shape," which suggests that increases in one dimension ought to be matched by increases in another dimension.

Allow some time for a free range of idea-sharing for Question 4. The same sort of ideas come up again in today's activity.

3. *How to Shrink It?*
(see page 48)

The purpose of today's activity, *How to Shrink It?*, is to help students further develop a sense of the conditions for polygons to be considered as having the same shape. They will look at what happens when one tries to shrink a drawing of a polygon by various methods:

- By subtracting a fixed amount from the lengths of each of its sides

- By dividing each of its angles by a fixed constant

- By dividing the lengths of each of its sides by a fixed constant

Some students may find this activity redundant in light of the homework discussion. Emphasize to them that, so far, they have no formal definition of "same shape," and so there are no simple answers yet.

You can challenge these students, or students that finish early, by drawing a vertical or horizontal line segment and asking them to make a drawing using this segment as a particular side of a house so that their drawing has the same shape as Renata's house.

You may want to mention that this activity is also intended to reinforce understanding of length and angle measurement, especially protractor use. Students who feel competent with their protractor can help someone who wants assistance.

How to Shrink It?

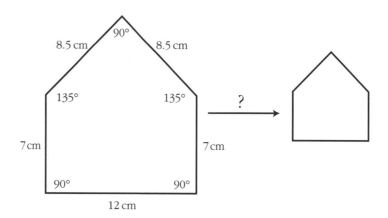

Lola, Lily, and Lulu love Renata's house, but find it a little too large for their liking.

In other words, they want to shrink the house down to a smaller size while keeping it exactly the same shape.

After a long discussion, each came up with a strategy for drawing the smaller house.

Lola's Way: Keep all the angles as they are and subtract five centimeters from the length of each side.

Lily's Way: Keep all the lengths as they are and divide all the angles by two.

Lulu's Way: Keep all the angles as they are and divide the lengths of all the sides by two.

Try to shrink the house by using each of the methods above. Show what result each method produces. Explain why the method does or does not work.

4. Discussion of *How to Shrink It?*

"Why will Lola's method work or not work? What about Lily's? What about Lulu's?"

You can begin by asking the class if anyone can explain why each method will or will not work. Use students' responses to gauge how much clarity and precision to press for.

For example, if a student says, "Lily's method won't work because the angles aren't the same as Renata's," ask why the angles need to be the same. As in the discussion of *Homework 6: Draw the Same Shape,* be alert for language that is leading up to the definition of similarity, because we want students to be moving toward articulation of this concept. (They will be given the formal definition tomorrow.)

This may be a time when students get frustrated, because they feel that they "know the answer" but cannot find the words to describe their thoughts. Encourage them to work on ways to say what they mean. You may want to give them some quiet time to try to write down their ideas, or some time to discuss the idea of "same shape" within their groups.

Homework 7: The Statue of Liberty's Nose
(see page 50)

This assignment gives another concrete setting in which to explore the idea of similarity. Students are likely to find that the concept of proportionality is a natural one to use in this context. The problem will be used to clarify the meaning of proportionality in the context of similar triangles.

• •

Homework 7   The Statue of Liberty's Nose

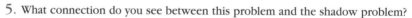

Consider this problem:

> The Statue of Liberty in New York City
> has a nose that is 4 feet 6 inches long.*
> What is the approximate length of
> one of her arms?

1. Solve the problem.
   (*Hint:* Think about your
   own nose and arms.)

2. Pick two other body
   parts and find the
   approximate length that
   these parts should be on
   the Statue of Liberty.

3. Examine what you did
   with the three examples
   from Questions 1 and 2.
   How was your work the
   same in the three cases? How
   did it change from case to
   case?

4. State how this problem is
   similar to the problem of
   drawing a house that has
   the same shape as another
   house (Question 2 from
   *Homework 6: Draw the
   Same Shape*).

5. What connection do you see between this problem and the shadow problem?

*Measurement taken from *How They Built the Statue of Liberty* by Mary Shapiro (Random House, 1985).

POW 16 Presentations and Defining Similarity

Students present POW 16 and learn the formal definition of similarity.

Mathematical Topics

• Spiralaterals

• Proportional reasoning

• Identifying corresponding parts of objects

• Defining similarity and congruence

Outline of the Day

In Class

1. Presentations of *POW 16: Spiralaterals*
   • Prod students to explain their observations

2. Discuss *Homework 7: The Statue of Liberty's Nose*
   • Focus on the use of ratios
   • Introduce the term **corresponding parts**

3. State and post the definition of **similarity**
   • Work through a simple example to illustrate the use of ratios

4. Review earlier activities involving the general concept of similarity
   • Introduce **congruence** as a special case of similarity

At Home

Homework 8: Make It Similar

POW 17: Cutting the Pie (due Day 14)

1. Presentations of POW 16: *Spiralaterals*

Ask the three students to make their POW presentations. As presenters share their observations about spiralaterals, prod them and the rest of the class to look for explanations.

"Why might sequences of length 4 be different from sequences of other lengths?"

For example, if students investigated the question of when a spiralateral returns to its starting point, they may have seen that sequences of length 2, 3, or 5 always return, but sequences of length 4 do not necessarily return. You can ask what it is about length 4 that makes these sequences different from others, and whether there are other lengths besides 4 for which sequences need not return to start.

After the initial presentations, ask other students to share any discoveries they made or any variations on the idea of spiralaterals that they investigated.

You may want to suggest areas of further exploration for interested students, for example:

• What happens if 0 is used in the sequence?

• Can negative numbers be used? What about fractions?

• How does the analysis change if the angle of turn is, say, 60°? If it is 120°?

2. Discussion of Homework 7: *The Statue of Liberty's Nose*

• *Questions 1 and 2*

Ask for volunteers to present Question 1 and some examples for Question 2. Presumably, this will be done by using ideas of proportionality, although students may not use such terminology. For example, a student might say something like, "The Statue of Liberty's nose is about 25 times as long as my nose, so the statue's arm should be about 25 times as long as my arm."

Note: Students may have different ways of measuring their noses or arms, so their results may not be the same. You may want to have a couple of students describe how they did their own body measurements.

•*For teacher's information: Two kinds of ratios*

There are, broadly speaking, two ways to use proportionality in Question 1. One approach, as just described, is to find the *nose to nose* ratio for the two figures (statue and person), and then apply that ratio to arms.

Another approach is to find the *arm to nose* ratio for a person, and then apply that ratio to the statue. For example, one might observe that the length of a person's arm is about 15 times the length of that person's nose, and conclude that the statue's

arm should be about 15 times the length of the statue's nose.

Students do *not* need to see both approaches. If only one of these approaches comes up, there is no need to introduce the other. This distinction will be discussed in connection with *Homework 16: Ins and Outs of Proportion.*

• *Questions 3 and 4*

Next turn to a general discussion of Questions 3 and 4 (which may overlap with each other).

The key idea connecting the Statue of Liberty problem to the "same shape" house problem (Question 2 of *Homework 6: Draw the Same Shape*) is that the Statue of Liberty is, more or less, the same shape as a person. You can use students' arithmetic procedures and language from the statue problem to help them understand the broader ideas.

If the language of ratio and proportion didn't emerge in the discussion of Questions 1 and 2 of the homework, you can try to elicit it in this discussion of Questions 3 and 4, introducing it yourself if needed.

For example, suppose a student uses the *arm to nose* approach described above (under the subheading "For teacher's information: Two kinds of ratios"). You can summarize this analysis by saying, "You saw that the **ratio** between the length of a person's arm and the length of a person's nose was about 15 to 1, so you wanted this ratio to be the same for the statue."

Tell students that when two ratios are the same, we say that the numbers involved are **proportional**, and that a statement that two ratios are the same is called a **proportion**.

Also use the term **corresponding parts** in summarizing what students did in the statue problem. For example, you can point out that the statue's nose and a person's nose are corresponding parts of the two objects. If students used the first approach to Question 1 described above (under the subheading "Questions 1 and 2"), point out that they were finding the ratio of corresponding parts.

"If the nose of the person and the nose of the statue are called corresponding parts, what would be corresponding parts in 'How to Shrink It?'"

You can ask what would be corresponding parts for the house problem. For instance, the *floor* of one house and the *floor* of another would be called corresponding parts of two house diagrams.

Try to get students to combine the terms *ratio, corresponding parts,* and *same shape* in a summary statement that is something like this:

When objects are the same shape, the ratio of the lengths for one pair of corresponding parts is the same as the ratio of the lengths for any other pair of corresponding parts.

Ask if students can state the above principle using the word *proportional.* Work with them to come up with a statement like this:

When objects are the same shape, corresponding parts are proportional in length.

It will be helpful if students can achieve this level of clarity in the context of a problem as concrete as the statue problem, so that they can use the language in the more abstract context of similar polygons.

• Question 5

Students may not see right away how the idea of *same shape* connects to the shadow problem, and Question 5 is intended to get them started in looking for the connections and looking for "same shapes" in the shadow problem.

These are deep and complex ideas, and it doesn't make sense to pursue them beyond what students can state on their own. So you may want to ask students what ideas they had on Question 5 and simply acknowledge their ideas with a nod, without discussing if they are right or wrong or pushing for a more complete discussion.

---

3. Defining Similarity

Tell the students that mathematicians use the term **similar** to describe objects that are the same shape. Emphasize that mathematicians are very specific as to what they mean when they refer to *same shape,* and that the definition you are giving them applies specifically to **polygons**.

You may want to state the definition using both the term *ratio* and the term *proportional,* so that students see the connection between the terms.

For example, you might state the definition in this way:

Two polygons (with the same number of sides) are similar if
- **their corresponding angles are equal, and**
- **their corresponding sides are proportional in length (that is, the ratios of the lengths of corresponding sides are equal)**

Post the definition prominently in the classroom. You may need to emphasize that *both* conditions must hold in order for two polygons to be considered similar. (If necessary, review what a polygon is. Students will have seen this term in the *Patterns* unit.)

You might point out that the word *similar* is used in ordinary language in a much more general sense, and that one needs to distinguish between that everyday use and this formal, mathematical definition.

You may want to point out explicitly that if two polygons don't have the same number of sides, then you can't set up corresponding sides and angles, so the polygons can't be similar.

Note: The concept of *corresponding parts* is hard to state concisely without introducing some notational formalism. Fortunately, it probably doesn't need belaboring, since students usually understand it intuitively. Use of the phrase *corresponding parts* in the context of the Statue of Liberty problem should be helpful. Tomorrow's discussion of tonight's homework will provide a good opportunity to dispel any confusion about corresponding sides.

• *A simple example*

Students may find it helpful to look at a simple example that illustrates how proportionality can be used. For instance, you can draw a pair of quadrilaterals, such as those below, with lengths labeled as indicated. Tell students to assume that the figures are similar, and ask them to find the lengths indicated by question marks.

"What are the missing lengths?"

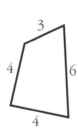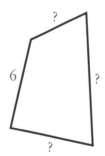

The main idea to develop is that the given side of the larger figure is 1.5 times the size of its corresponding part, so this same ratio must apply to all the other pairs of corresponding sides.

4. Looking Back at Question 3 of *Homework 6: Draw the Same Shape*

With this formal definition of similarity in place, ask students to look back at the pairs of figures in Question 3 of *Homework 6: Draw the Same Shape,* and to reach consensus in their groups about whether each pair of figures is similar or not.

They should see that the pairs in Question 3a and in Question 3d are similar and that the pairs in Question 3b and in Question 3c are not.

• *Orientation*

Discussion of Question 3a should include the issue of the **orientation** of a figure. Although this may play a role in the students' intuitive concept of shape, it is not part of the mathematician's definition of similarity. That is, turning a figure does not change its shape, according to the definition of similarity.

Question 3d brings up another aspect of orientation, since these two triangles are **mirror images** of each other. Students should be told, if needed, that the mirror image of a figure is considered similar to the figure itself.

It should be emphasized that the way one deals with this issue of orientation is simply a matter of *convention*—that is, an agreement on terminology by mathematicians. If students think that these pairs of figures have different shapes, that's okay. They are not wrong to think that, but they do have to understand the technical way that the word *similar* is used in mathematics.

• *Congruence*

Question 3a should also bring up the fact that similar figures do not have to be different sizes. Tell students that similar figures in which corresponding sides are actually *equal* in length (that is, where the ratio of corresponding sides is equal to 1) are called **congruent**.

You can use Question 3d to clarify students' understanding of the phrase *corresponding parts*. For instance, you can point to a side of one of the triangles and ask students what the corresponding side is in the other triangle.

• *More on corresponding parts*

Although the figures in Question 3c are not similar, they can be used to clarify the concepts of proportionality and corresponding parts. You can ask students what parts might be considered to be *corresponding.* They will presumably consider the two bases corresponding parts and the sides corresponding parts.

Then have students measure these corresponding parts of the two triangles and find the ratio for each pair. They should see that for one pair (the bases), the ratio is 1, but for the other two pairs, the ratio is something else.

It is important that the proportional sides and equal angles be corresponding parts. A supplemental problem (*How Can They Not Be Similar?*) asks students to construct two polygons for which the sides of the first are actually equal to the sides of the second and the angles of the first are equal to the angles of the second, but the figures are not similar.

Homework 8: Make It Similar
(see page 58)

This homework will clarify the concept of corresponding sides and give students some experience working with proportions.

POW 17: Cutting the Pie
(see page 59)

This POW involves a fairly complex pattern-analysis of a geometrical problem. Most students will be able to gather some data, and many will see a sequential pattern in the data.

The additional step of finding a general formula will probably be difficult for most students, and understanding why that formula fits the geometry of the problem is yet another dimension of the POW.

Discussion of this POW is scheduled for Day 14.

Homework 8   Make It Similar

You have seen that two polygons are called **similar** if their corresponding angles are equal and their corresponding sides are proportional.

The phrase "corresponding sides are proportional" means that if you compare each side of the first polygon to the corresponding side in the second polygon, the ratios of those lengths are all the same.

Here's a problem where you need to think carefully about which sides are corresponding.

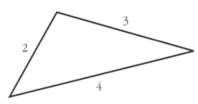

First, suppose you have one triangle whose sides have lengths of 2 inches, 3 inches, and 4 inches, as shown at the right.

Next, suppose there is a second triangle that is known to be similar to the first one.

And suppose you know that one of the sides of this larger triangle is 6 inches long.

Unfortunately, you don't know which side of the large triangle has this length.

What can you say about the lengths of the other sides of the larger triangle? Try to find all the possibilities. (There's more than one answer. Don't assume that the triangles shown are drawn to scale.)

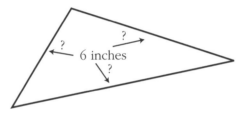

POW 17   Cutting the Pie

You can sometimes organize information from experiments into In-Out tables to help you understand what's happening in the experiment.

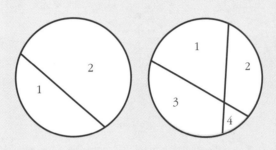

The diagrams to the left show the results of a pie-cutting experiment. In the first picture, one cut across the pie has created two pieces. In the next diagram, two cuts have created a total of four pieces.

Notice that the cuts do not necessarily go through the center of the pie, but they do have to be straight and go all the way across the pie. Also, the pieces do not have to be the same size or shape.

The two diagrams below show different possible results from making three cuts in the pie.

In the first case, the three cuts produced six pieces, while in the second case, the three cuts produced seven pieces. (It's also possible to produce five or even only four pieces from three cuts.)

You should be able to convince yourself that seven is the largest number of pieces that can be created by three cuts across the pie.

The purpose of the pie-cutting experiment is to find out:

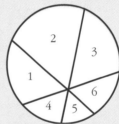 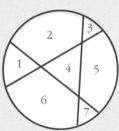

What is the largest number of pieces that can be produced from a given number of cuts?

Continued on next page

The information from the diagrams on the previous page has been organized into the In-Out table below. Your task is to extend and analyze this table.

1. Find the largest number of pieces you can get from four cuts and from five cuts. Include those numbers in your table.

Number of cuts	Maximum number of pieces
1	2
2	4
3	7
4	?
5	?

2. a. Try to find a pattern describing what is happening in the table.

   b. Use your pattern to find the largest possible number of pieces from ten cuts.

   c. Try to explain *why* this pattern is occurring.

3. Try to find a rule for the In-Out table. That is, if you used a variable for the input, how could you write the output as a formula in terms of that variable?

Write-up

1. *Problem statement*

2. *Process:* Include important diagrams you used while working on this problem.

3. *Solution:* This should include

   • your In-Out table (as far as you took it)

   • any patterns you found in the table, expressed either in words or in symbols (or both)

   • your answer for the largest possible number of pieces from ten cuts

   • explanations for your answers

4. *Evaluation*

Similarity and Counterexamples

Students explore the two parts of the definition of similarity to see if both conditions are needed.

Mathematical Topics

- Recognizing corresponding sides in similar figures
- Expressing proportionality of sides by using equations
- Use of counterexamples
- Examining the conditions for similarity

Outline of the Day

In Class

1. Discuss *Homework 8: Make It Similar*
   - Focus on the term **corresponding sides**
2. Notation for polygons and similarity
   - Introduce the naming of polygons by their vertices
   - Introduce the symbol ~ for similarity
   - Introduce the notation $\overline{PQ}$ for a line segment and PQ for the length of the segment
3. *Is There a Counterexample?*
   - Identify the two parts of the definition of similarity

- Review the concept of a *counterexample* and its relationship to "If . . . , then . . . " statements
- Optional: Introduce the terms **hypothesis** and **conclusion**
- Students will look for counterexamples to statements about similarity

4. Discuss *Is There a Counterexample?*
   - Students should see that both conditions in the definition of similarity are needed

At Home

Homework 9: Triangular Counterexamples

Discuss With Your Colleagues

Counterexamples and Logic

Although this unit does not use the traditional, axiomatic approach to geometry, it does afford students opportunities to work with fundamentals of formal logic, such as "If . . . , then . . ." statements and counterexamples.

What is the proper role of this formalism in the high school curriculum? How does the type of experience with logic in this unit help students learn to think clearly? How does this experience compare with what they would get from the axiomatic approach?

1. Discussion of *Homework 8: Make It Similar*

Discussion of this assignment provides a good opportunity to clarify the concept of *corresponding sides*.

"How many solutions did you find?"

You might begin by asking how many solutions students found. Before getting into the details of any one solution, you can have students explain why there was more than one.

It may help to refer to the diagrams of the two triangles in the assignment, perhaps drawing them side by side, as shown below.

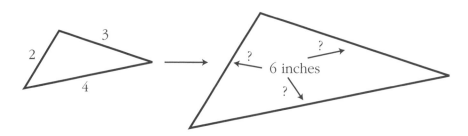

"Exactly what did you do to find the lengths of the other sides?"

Then you can ask for volunteers to describe in detail how they did the arithmetic of finding the other sides for one of the three cases.

Note: The case where the 6-inch side is the longest side of the new triangle may be more difficult, since in this case the ratio of corresponding sides is not a whole number. You might want to discuss this case explicitly.

If possible, get students to articulate the need to find the ratio of the sides from one triangle to another. One objective of this activity is for them to learn to set up problems like these as proportions.

> For example, using the case where the 6-inch side of the second triangle is the longest side, the reasoning may be expressed something like this:
>
> The 6-inch side of the second triangle corresponds to the 4-inch side of the original triangle, so the ratio of corresponding sides is 6 to 4. Therefore, the same ratio applies to other pairs of sides. To find the length of the side of the second triangle corresponding to the 2-inch side of the original triangle, one needs to solve the equation $\frac{x}{2} = \frac{6}{4}$.

Identify an equation such as $\frac{x}{2} = \frac{6}{4}$ as a **proportion**. (Although this word has been used before, this may be the first time students see it in the context of a formal equation.) You may want to point out that it says that two fractions—that is, *ratios*—are equal.

"Are there other ways to set up a proportion for this problem?"

Keep in mind that there are many ways to set up the proportion, and urge students to present alternatives.

Discuss with students how they would go about getting a solution to such an equation.

> At this point, we are not expecting them to use formal algebra techniques, just their intuition about numbers. Don't teach them rules like "cross-multiply." However, encourage them to check their answers, using a calculator if appropriate. (*Note:* In *Homework 10: Similar Problems,* students will get further work on setting up proportions, and in *Homework 13: Inventing Rules,* they will investigate ways to solve proportions.)
>
> Students might not use equations to solve the problem. For example, they may get their answers by saying something like, "The big triangle is $1\frac{1}{2}$ times as big as the small one, so just multiply all three sides by $1\frac{1}{2}$." If so, you can identify the number $1\frac{1}{2}$ as "the ratio of corresponding sides."

• *Optional: An alternate equation*

Rather than look at ratios *between corresponding sides,* some students may see that the ratio of two sides *within the original triangle* must be equal to the corresponding ratio in the new triangle. For example, the "short-side-to-long-side" ratio in the original triangle is 2 to 4, so this ratio must also apply in the second triangle.

Based on this reasoning, a student would come up with an equation like

$$\frac{x}{6} = \frac{2}{4}$$

to find the short side of the second triangle (for the case where the 6-inch side is the longest side of the second triangle).

This is equivalent to the earlier equation, but reflects a different approach. If it doesn't come up, you need not raise it. This idea is discussed in *Homework 16: Ins and Outs of Proportion* and is used in connection with the development of the trigonometric ratios.

2. Digression: Notation for Polygons and Similarity

This is a good time to take a few minutes to discuss notation for the naming of polygons and for similarity.

Start with the idea of naming a polygon by its vertices (although some students may be familiar with this).

For example, draw a polygon and label its vertices as shown below, and tell students that this figure can be referred to as "pentagon *ABCDE*."

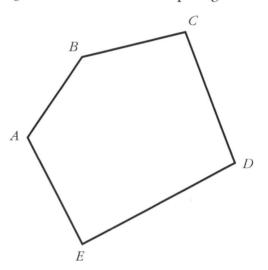

"What other names might you give this polygon?"

Ask students for other names they might give this polygon. Be sure they see that they can go in either direction around the figure and can start anywhere. (For example, they can call this figure *DCBAE*.) They should realize, however, that the sequence of letters has to match the way the vertices are connected. (For example, they *cannot* call the figure *ABCED*.)

Also draw a triangle with labeled vertices, and introduce the use of the triangle symbol as an abbreviation. For example, the triangle below can be represented in writing as △*PQR*.

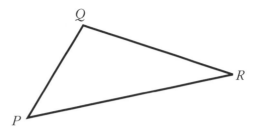

"What other names might you use for this triangle?"

As was done with the pentagon, ask students for other names for this figure. They should see that it can also be called △*PRQ*, △*QPR*, and so on.

Next, introduce the symbol ~ to represent similarity, and illustrate with an example such as the following, reading the symbols aloud by stating, "Triangle *PQR* is similar to triangle *STU*."

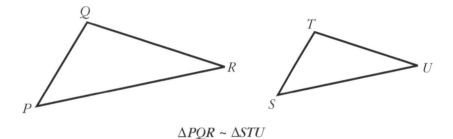

△*PQR* ~ △*STU*

Point out that the notation △*PQR* ~ △*STU* not only states that the triangles are similar, but also indicates how the vertices correspond. For example, students should *not* write △*PQR* ~ △*SUT*, since that would suggest that *Q* and *U* were corresponding vertices. (Don't get too caught up in the technicalities here, though.)

This is also a good time to introduce geometric notation for lines, segments, and rays. The notation given below is fairly standard, but not universal. We will be using this notation as needed in both teacher and student materials.

- The **line** through two points *A* and *B* will be written as $\overleftrightarrow{AB}$.

- The **line segment** connecting *A* and *B* will be written as $\overline{AB}$, and the **length** of this segment will be written as *AB*.

- The **ray** from *A* through *B* will be written as $\overrightarrow{AB}$.

Make sure students realize that *AB* is not a product of two variables.

3. *Is There a Counterexample?*
(see page 69)

The next activity, *Is There a Counterexample?*, has two primary purposes:

- To give students insight into the two parts of the definition of similarity

- To strengthen students' understanding of basic concepts of mathematical logic, including review of the term *counterexample* (introduction of the formal terms *hypothesis* and *conclusion* is optional)

"Who can state the definition of similarity?"

You can introduce the activity by asking for a volunteer to restate the definition of similar polygons. You should be able to get a statement like this:

Two polygons are similar if their corresponding angles are equal and their corresponding sides are proportional.

Point out that there are two conditions in this definition—*equal corresponding angles* and *proportional corresponding sides*—and tell students that their next activity involves investigating the two parts of the definition.

Specifically, point out that they saw that figures with "the same shape" do have both properties. The essence of the activity is for them to see if it's possible for a pair of figures to be "half similar," that is, for a pair of figures to have one of these properties but not the other.

• *More about counterexamples*

Students already have seen and used the term *counterexample* in *Patterns* (primarily in connection with their work on consecutive sums), and they may have looked at the "If . . . , then . . ." form that many mathematical generalizations take.

However, they may still be somewhat uncomfortable with such formalism, so use your judgment about whether to discuss "If . . . , then . . ." statements before students get started on the activity, or whether to let them get to work on the geometry and clarify the logic as they work.

Using examples is probably the best way to review what a counterexample is. For instance, give them this statement and ask them if it's true:

All odd numbers are primes.

Students will probably know that this statement is false.

"How do you know this is false? Be specific."

Next ask for a specific number that shows that the statement is false. When you get such a number, such as 9 or 15, ask what that number is called in this context. If necessary, remind students of the term **counterexample**.

"What exactly makes that number a counterexample?"

Ask students to explain in detail what it is about the given number that makes it a counterexample to the above statement. For example, they should be able to say something like, "The number 9 is a counterexample because it's odd but it's not a prime."

"Which of these numbers are counterexamples? Why?"

You can pursue this further with questions such as the following:

- Is 7 a counterexample? Why or why not?

- Is 6 a counterexample? Why or why not?

- Is 2 a counterexample? Why or why not?

• *"If . . . , then . . ." statements*

The statement used above, "All odd numbers are primes," is not stated in the formal "If . . . , then . . ." mode, and it is important for students to see mathematical assertions in different syntactical forms. But they should also gradually become familiar with this special way of making mathematical statements. Here is an example you might want to use as an illustration.

If a number is even, then it is a multiple of 4.

Again, get students to articulate that the statement is false, to give a counterexample (such as 6 or 10), and to explain why the given number is a counterexample. For example, they should be able to say that 6 is a counterexample because it is even, but it's not a multiple of 4.

Point out that when mathematicians use "If . . . , then . . ." language, they intend it as a universal statement; that is, it is supposed to apply to *all* even numbers.

"How could you phrase that statement without using 'If . . . , then . . .' ?"

You might ask students for other ways to make the statement (making sure they realize that the statement is false).

Here are some illustrations of responses you might get.

"Whenever any number is even, then that number must be a multiple of 4."

"All even numbers are multiples of 4."

• *Statement 1 of "Is There a Counterexample?"*

If it seems necessary, have students articulate what would be needed to have a counterexample for Statement 1 of the activity. They should see that they are looking for a pair of polygons that have their corresponding angles equal, but that are not similar.

Don't be afraid to give students hints if they seem stuck. If they are working with triangles for Statements 1 and 2 of the activity, encourage them to try polygons with more sides. Also encourage them to work with familiar angles, such as right angles.

• *Optional: Hypothesis and conclusion*

You may want to introduce the terms **hypothesis** and **conclusion** for the "if" and "then" parts of statements like those just discussed, and to ask students to use this language to explain what a counterexample is.

Help them as needed to see that a counterexample is an object that fits the hypothesis but does not fit the conclusion; that is, it makes the hypothesis true and makes the conclusion false.

Note: Students are probably more accustomed to the meaning of the word *hypothesis* in the scientific context, in which it generally describes a conjecture about how something works. For example, in *The Pit and the Pendulum,* students made the hypothesis that the period of a pendulum is a function of its length, and they used that hypothesis to estimate the period of a 30-foot pendulum. If you introduce the terms *hypothesis* and *conclusion* here, you may want to clarify that the word *hypothesis* has a somewhat different meaning in logic from its meaning in science.

4. Discussion of *Is There a Counterexample?*

Have the first few groups that finish prepare overhead transparencies of their counterexamples. When they are ready, stop the class and have them present their findings.

It will be easier to begin with Statements 1 and 2, for which there are counterexamples.

The simplest counterexamples are probably these:

- For Statement 1: a square and a nonsquare rectangle
- For Statement 2: a square and a nonsquare rhombus

Keep in mind, though, that students may find more exotic counterexamples.

Is There a Counterexample?

Try to find counterexamples for each of the statements below by creating appropriate pairs of polygons.

If you think you have found a counterexample, explain why your pair of polygons disproves the given statement.

If you think that there is no counterexample for a given statement, explain why you think so.

Reminder: Not every polygon is a triangle, so be sure to consider figures with more than three sides.

Statement 1

If two polygons have their corresponding angles equal, then the polygons are similar.

Statement 2

If two polygons have their corresponding sides proportional, then the polygons are similar.

Statement 3

Every triangle with two equal sides also has two equal angles.

Interactive Mathematics Program

Ask the presenting groups how they knew that they had a counterexample. Make sure they verify both that the polygons fit the hypothesis and that they are not similar.

Specifically, go over how to check the proportionality of sides. Ideally, this should come from the presenters. However, they may have counterexamples that are obviously dissimilar and may therefore see no need to check the proportionality of the side lengths.

• *Statement 3*

In the case of Statement 3, students will probably believe that there are no counterexamples, but may be unsure how to articulate this. They should realize that if there really are no counterexamples, then the statement is true.

Bring out clearly that *not finding a counterexample* is not the same as *none existing*. In other words, the fact that they didn't find a counterexample does not mean they have proved that the statement is true.

You should assure students that Statement 3 is actually true. Let them talk about what makes them think so. They may be able to give a good intuitive explanation based on symmetry.

Homework 9: Triangular Counterexamples
(see facing page)

Tonight's homework is similar to the activity *Is There a Counterexample?* Statements 1 and 3 are both true and are important ideas for students to understand intuitively. Their experience in looking for counterexamples should lead them to a strong feeling that the statements are true.

Activities on Days 10 and 11 will help them see why these statements are true.

Homework 9   Triangular Counterexamples

Attempt to draw counterexamples to each of the following statements. Be sure to show all your work, including any appropriate diagrams.

If you don't think a counterexample exists, then explain why you think there isn't one.

Statement 1

If two triangles have their corresponding angles equal, then the triangles are similar.

Statement 2

If two triangles are both isosceles, then the triangles are similar.

(*Reminder:* An isosceles triangle is a triangle with at least two sides of equal length.)

Statement 3

If two triangles have their corresponding sides proportional, then the triangles are similar.

Interactive Mathematics Program   423

Days 10-16

Triangles Galore

The unit now moves from polygons in general to triangles in particular, but algebra starts playing an important role as well. You will be investigating the special case of triangles in more detail, using angles, parallel lines, and ratios.

This page in the student book introduces Days 10 through 16

While you investigate these ideas, you might keep thinking about the unit problem that's waiting for you in the shadows, and ask yourself what triangles and equations have to do with it.

Tamika Greene demonstrates how she might make a specific triangle using straws.

424

Interactive Mathematics Program

Why Are Triangles Special?

Students discover the "rigidity" of triangles and see why it's easier to prove similarity for triangles than for other polygons.

Mathematical Topics

- Continued work with counterexamples
- Learning through experiment that triangles with the same set of side lengths are congruent, and developing an intuitive understanding of why this is so

Outline of the Day

In Class

1. Progress report on *POW 17: Cutting the Pie*
   - Confirm that students have found the right values for 4 and 5 cuts
2. Discuss *Homework 9: Triangular Counterexamples*
   - Focus on the fact that only one of the conditions on similarity seems to be needed for triangles

3. *Why Are Triangles Special?*
   - Students investigate the rigidity of triangles by using physical models
4. Discuss *Why Are Triangles Special?*
   - Clarify and post the principle that the lengths of the sides of a triangle determine the triangle up to congruence

At Home

Homework 10: Similar Problems

Special Materials Needed

You should provide materials for constructing triangles such as

- Straws (10 per group)
- Dental floss (preferably unwaxed) or string—several feet per group
- Scissors—one per group

Discuss With Your Colleagues

Axioms or Experiments?

Today's activity, *Why Are Triangles Special?*, revolves around the principle that the lengths of the sides of a triangle determine the triangle up to congruence. In other words, two triangles with the same set of side lengths must be congruent (and hence similar).

In traditional geometry courses, this principle is either an axiom or a theorem (the "SSS" principle), but in this unit, it is primarily seen as an experimental observation. (The treatment of principles for parallel lines is similar—see Day 15.)

Discuss with your colleagues, combining your present experience in IMP with your previous experience, how students have reacted to the two different approaches. Which gives them a better understanding of the physical world or a better appreciation of Euclid's own insights?

1. Progress Report on *POW 17: Cutting the Pie*

"What maximum did you find for 4 cuts? For 5 cuts?"

This is a good time to check that students are making progress on their POW. You should confirm that they understand what the In-Out table is supposed to record. You may want to verify that they have at least found the correct maximum number of pieces for the cases of 4 cuts and 5 cuts.

Having this information confirmed should allow students to focus on the more interesting and challenging aspects of the POW—looking for a pattern to the table, using that pattern to find the *Out* for a large *In,* trying to explain the pattern, and looking for an algebraic rule to describe the pattern.

2. Discussion of *Homework 9: Triangular Counterexamples*

"Did you find any counterexamples?"

Ask the class if anyone was able to find any counterexamples for the homework. Presumably, most of them will have found counterexamples for Statement 2.

Go over one or two of these counterexamples, to solidify the idea of what a counterexample is.

• Statements 1 and 3

"What about for Statement 1? For Statement 3?"

Ask specifically if anyone found counterexamples to Statements 1 and 3 of the homework. If someone has a proposed counterexample, have the class look at it. They should check whether the triangles use the same three angles and whether corresponding sides are proportional. (It could be that someone thought they had a counterexample to Statement 1 because they checked the proportions of noncorresponding sides.)

You should be able to arrive at the conclusion that no one found a legitimate counterexample to either Statement 1 or Statement 3.

"What does it mean if you didn't find a counterexample?"

Ask the class what this lack of a counterexample tells them. They should see that this does *not* mean that the statements are true (although it does seem like a strong suggestion). The fact that they have not *found* a counterexample does not guarantee that there isn't one.

If there were students who did not find a counterexample for Statement 2, you can ask the class if those students would have been correct in deducing that Statement 2 was true.

You should, however, assure students that Statements 1 and 3 are both true, and tell them that the next activity, *Why Are Triangles Special?*, and tomorrow's activity, *Are Angles Enough?*, should give them some further intuitive understanding of why.

3. Why Are Triangles Special?
(see next page)

"How do Statements 1 and 2 from 'Is There a Counterexample?' compare to Statements 1 and 3 of the homework?"

Once students have a sense that Statements 1 and 3 seem to be true, have them compare those two statements with Statements 1 and 2 from *Is There a Counterexample?*

They should come up with this comparison.

(From *Homework 9: Triangular Counterexamples*)	(From the Day 9 activity, *Is There a Counterexample?*)
Statement 1	**Statement 1**
If two triangles have their corresponding angles equal, then the triangles are similar.	If two polygons have their corresponding angles equal, then the polygons are similar.
TRUE	FALSE
Statement 3	**Statement 2**
If two triangles have their corresponding sides proportional, then the triangles are similar.	If two polygons have their corresponding sides proportional, then the polygons are similar.
TRUE	FALSE

So there seems to be something about triangles that allows one to conclude that they are similar with less information than is needed for polygons in general.

Tell students that their next activity will help them see what makes triangles so special. It will help explain why, for triangles, they only need to meet one of the two conditions for similarity, while for polygons in general, they need to meet both.

Why Are Triangles Special?

You have seen that triangles seem to be different from other polygons with regard to similarity.

In this activity, you will investigate why triangles are special.

1. Pick four lengths and form a quadrilateral using those lengths for the sides of a quadrilateral.

   Then try to use the same four lengths to form a quadrilateral that is not similar to the first. Can you?

2. Repeat Question 1 starting with more than four lengths. That is, pick some lengths and form a polygon using those lengths; then, using the same lengths, try to form a polygon that is not similar to the first.

3. Start with three lengths and use them to form a triangle. As in Questions 1 and 2, try to use the same lengths to form a triangle that is not similar to the first. Can you?

Pass out materials—such as straws, scissors, and dental floss (or string)—to the groups. Suggest that students cut the straws to different lengths to represent the sides of a quadrilateral. Demonstrate how to feed dental floss through the pieces of straw one after another so that the ends of the straws are adjacent, forming a flexible sequence of line segments. One can then tie the two ends of the dental floss together so that the straws create a model of a polygon.

4. Discussion of *Why Are Triangles Special?*

Let students discuss their observations from their investigation.

In using the materials, they should see that once they choose lengths and make a polygon, the triangle has a kind of "rigidity" that is absent in polygons with more than three sides. This lack of rigidity in polygons with more than three sides is sometimes called "play."

Students will see that they cannot make different triangles from a given set of lengths, but if there are more than three sides, then many different-shaped polygons can be built with those lengths for the sides of the polygon.

Review the term *congruent* (introduced on Day 8) for two polygons that are the same shape and size. In other words, two polygons are congruent if they are similar and if the ratio of corresponding sides is equal to 1.

"Can you state what you learned in the activity, using the idea of congruence?"

Ask if students can restate what they discovered in the activity in terms of congruence. If a hint is needed, ask students what would be true of the triangles formed if one student used the same three lengths as another student. With help, they should be able to make a statement like this:

If the sides of one triangle have the same lengths as the corresponding sides of another triangle, then the triangles must be congruent.

You may want to post this statement. This principle is also expressed by saying that the set of lengths of the sides **determines a triangle**.

Bring out that this principle does not hold in general for polygons:

If the sides of one polygon have the same lengths as the corresponding sides of another polygon, then the polygons do not have to be congruent.

Ask how this special characteristic of triangles relates to similarity. You may need to bring out that two triangles having the same set of lengths as each other (as in the above principle about triangles) is a special case of having the sides of one triangle proportional to the sides of the other—it is the special case where the ratio of corresponding sides is equal to 1.

Tell students that this distinction between triangles and other polygons— that triangles are rigid and polygons in general are not—is essentially the reason why Statement 3 in last night's homework is, in fact, correct:

If two triangles have their corresponding sides proportional, then the triangles must be similar.

Students will look at Statement 1 of last night's homework (involving angles) as part of tomorrow's work.

Optional: Ask the class about the significance of this discussion for architecture and construction techniques. A supplemental problem on this subject, *Rigidity Can Be Good,* is included in this unit.

Homework 10 Similar Problems

In each of the four pairs of figures below, assume that the second polygon is similar to the first. In each case, do these steps:

- Set up equations to find the lengths of any sides labeled by variables.

- Find the length that solves each equation.

- Explain how you found the solutions to the equations.

Note: Measuring the diagrams will probably not give correct answers, because the diagrams may not be drawn exactly to scale.

1.

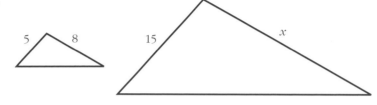

2.

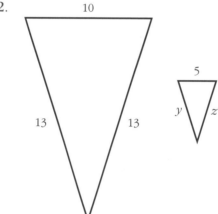

Continued on next page

Homework 10: Similar Problems

This homework is intended to give students practice in formalizing their work with proportionality. They are asked to write equations to represent each situation and then solve the equations to find the missing lengths.

3.

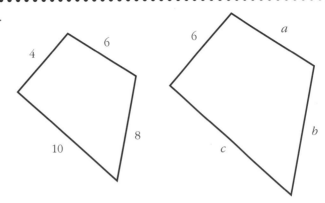

4.

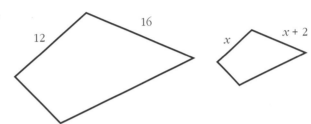

(*Note*: The side labeled $x + 2$ must be 2 units longer than the side labeled x.)

You may want to discuss the "Note" in the homework about measuring the diagrams.

Angles and Similarity

Students see that having corresponding angles equal is enough to guarantee similarity for triangles.

Mathematical Topics

- Working with similar triangles and proportions
- Learning from experiments that triangles with the same set of angles are similar, and developing an intuitive understanding of why this is so

• •

Outline of the Day

In Class

1. Discuss *Homework 10: Similar Problems*
   - Focus on setting up appropriate equations
2. *Are Angles Enough?*
   - Students investigate whether the shape of a triangle is determined by its angles

3. Discuss *Are Angles Enough?*
   - Clarify and post the principle that the angles of a triangle determine the triangle up to similarity

At Home

Homework 11: From Top to Bottom

1. Discussion of *Homework 10: Similar Problems*

You can give students a few minutes to compare their equations and solutions in groups, and then have spade card students present individual problems. You might choose to have each group pick a homework problem to present to the entire class (limit two groups per problem).

"How did you go about setting up equations?"

This is the first time in the unit that students have been asked to set up formal equations for their proportions, so you should give them an opportunity to discuss how they went about this.

> Keep in mind that there is more than one way to set up an appropriate equation. For example, any of the following equations can be used to express Question 1:
>
> $$\frac{x}{8} = \frac{15}{5} \qquad\qquad \frac{5}{15} = \frac{8}{x} \qquad\qquad \frac{5}{8} = \frac{15}{x}$$
>
> *Note:* The last of these equations equates ratios from within each triangle rather than ratios between corresponding sides of the triangles. *Homework 16: Ins and Outs of Proportion* will look at this idea.

"How did you solve the equations?"

In looking at the step of solving the equations, focus on the different ways that students solve the proportion equations. They will probably still work primarily with intuitive methods, including trial and error.

"How could you check that the solution is correct?"

Whatever approach is used to find the solution, you should insist that students verify that the suggested solution satisfies the equation by finding the value of each ratio. (*Note: Homework 13: Inventing Rules* continues this work in solving proportions.)

• *Cross-multiplication*

If any students suggest cross-multiplying as a method for solving proportions, you can acknowledge the correctness of this technique, without getting into questions for now of why this technique is correct, and move on to other methods as well. Working with cross-multiplication is suggested as part of the discussion of *Homework 13: Inventing Rules*.

2. *Are Angles Enough?*
(see facing page)

Students now have seen (at least experimentally) that having corresponding sides proportional guarantees similarity for triangles.

You can review this fact and ask the class to return to Statement 1 from *Homework 9: Triangular Counterexamples* ("If corresponding angles are equal, then triangles are similar"), perhaps having a student tell what they concluded about that statement.

Then have students work on the activity *Are Angles Enough?*

After Question 1, you may want to have some students trace each of their triangles onto transparencies so you can display them. You should choose examples of different sizes. If you then orient the transparencies so the angles match up, and superimpose the transparencies, students can "Oooh" and "Aaah" over the way the triangles nest inside one another. This gives a vivid, visual confirmation of the similarity of the triangles.

Are Angles Enough?

You've seen that the lengths of the sides of a triangle *determine* the triangle. Another way to say this is

> **If the lengths of the three sides of one triangle are the same as the lengths of the three sides of a second triangle, then the two triangles are congruent.**

What about angles? Do the *angles* of a triangle determine the triangle? In other words, what happens if two triangles have the same three angles as each other?

1. Start with angles of 40°, 60°, and 80°. Each group member should try to draw a triangle using these three angles.

   Did the triangles all come out congruent? Were they all similar? Why or why not?

Continued on next page

2. Next, do the same thing starting with a different set of angles. You might just draw some arbitrary triangle and then have each group member use the same angles as that triangle.

   Did the triangles all come out congruent? Were they all similar? Why or why not?

3. Now go back to the angles of 40°, 60°, and 80°. This time, decide as a group on the length each group member will use for the side connecting the angles of 40° and 60°. As before, have each group member try to draw a triangle using angles 40°, 60°, and 80°, but also using the given length in the given position.

   Did the triangles all come out congruent? Were they all similar? Why or why not?

4. What do these experiments suggest concerning Statement 1 of *Homework 9: Triangular Counterexamples*? Explain.

3. Discussion of *Are Angles Enough?*

Students should see that there was a kind of "rigidity" in this activity like that in yesterday's *Why Are Triangles Special?* Although students can vary the size of the triangles in Question 1, the shape of the triangle is determined. And once they pick one of the lengths involved, they have no choices about the rest of the triangle.

Again, post the general principle:

> **If two triangles have their corresponding angles equal, then the triangles must be similar.**

Some students may realize that only two pairs of corresponding angles need to be equals; that is, if two triangles have two pairs of their corresponding angles equal, then the triangles are similar. If this comes up, let students explain their reasoning. If not, it will be discussed on Day 13 (see the section "Two Angles for Similarity").

Homework 11: *From Top to Bottom*

(see next page)

Tonight's homework is an exercise in planning that requires students to think about proportional length.

You can get students started by having them work in their groups to measure various parts of the given pentagon. This should stimulate their thinking about how to go about making the desired scale drawings.

This assignment may be difficult for many students. Some students may develop general principles about scale drawing that make the work easier, and the discussion tomorrow can be used to help other students understand more about scale drawing.

• •

Homework 11   From Top to Bottom

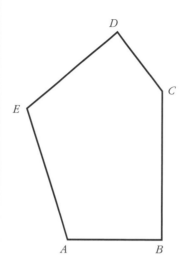

A scale drawing of a figure or object is a drawing that is *similar* to the original. In this assignment, you are to make two scale drawings of the pentagon *ABCDE,* which is shown at the left.

In each of your drawings, you are to keep the pentagon facing the same way it is shown at the left.

Make your two drawings on an $8\frac{1}{2}$-inch by 11-inch sheet of paper (standard binder paper), with one drawing on each side of the sheet.

Use a ruler and protractor to measure the sides and the angles carefully, in order to make your drawings as accurate as you can.

1. First make a scale drawing of the pentagon so that the bottom of it is one inch from the bottom of the sheet and the top of it is one inch from the top of the paper. Your drawing should be positioned roughly like the diagram at the right.

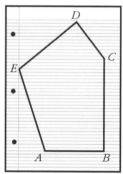

2. For your second drawing, flip the sheet of paper over and turn it sideways. With the paper in this position, again make a scale drawing of the pentagon.

   Again, the bottom of the pentagon should be one inch from the bottom of the sheet and the top of the pentagon should be one inch from the top of the paper, so that the pentagon is positioned roughly like the diagram at the right.

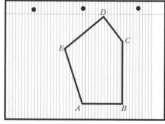

3. a. For each of your two drawings, find the ratio between the length of a side of your drawing and the length of the corresponding side in the actual pentagon in this assignment.

   b. How might you find these ratios before you start the drawings?

DAY 12 *Triangular Possibilities*

Students explore two crucial properties of triangles: angle sum and the triangle inequality.

Mathematical Topics

- Creating scale drawings
- Reviewing angle sum formulas for polygons
- Discovering the triangle inequality and looking for related properties for other polygons

Outline of the Day

In Class

1. Discuss *Homework 11: From Top to Bottom*

2. Discuss the connection between similar triangles and the unit problem

3. *What's Possible?*
   - Students investigate possibilities for angles and side lengths for triangles and try to generalize to other polygons

- The activity will be discussed on Day 13

At Home

Homework 12: Very Special Triangles

Special Materials Needed

- Scissors—one per group
- Straws—one per pair of students

1. Discussion of *Homework 11: From Top to Bottom*

"How did you get started on this problem?"

Ask two or three volunteers to talk about how they got started on this problem.

For example, one approach is to start with point B one inch from the bottom, estimate how far up to go in drawing $\overline{BC}$, and then draw $\overline{CD}$ proportionately and see if D comes out an inch from the top.

"Could you have found any measurements for the polygons in Questions 1 and 2 without trial and error?"

Then let volunteers give their ideas on Question 3. If no one has an idea, you can ask if there are any measurements of the polygons that students must draw that they can find without trial and error.

They should see, for example, that in Question 1, the vertical segment from D to $\overline{AB}$ must be 9 inches long. They can measure the same segment for the pentagon in the assignment to get a ratio that must be used for the lengths of the sides as well.

The general idea is that, in similar figures, not only are the lengths of corresponding sides proportional, but the lengths of *any* corresponding segments (such as these vertical segments, diagonals, and so forth) are also proportional.

Note: A supplemental problem, *Proportions Everywhere*, gives students a chance to explore this idea.

2. Reminder: What About Shadows?

Students may be wondering what happened to the unit problem. This is a good time to ask them to take a few minutes to do focused free-writing on this question:

> *What does the topic of similar triangles have to do with shadows?*

You may want to remind them of the diagram created on Day 3, which will probably look something like this:

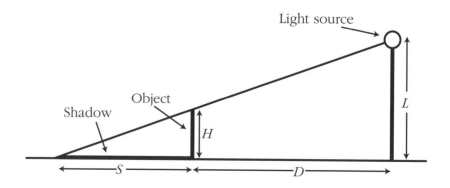

Probably many students will see that there are similar triangles in this diagram. But this is not the time to push ahead and solve the problem (although perhaps some students could do that now).

Rather, just use this occasion to assure them that the unit problem has not been forgotten and that the concept of similarity is relevant.

3. *What's Possible?*
(see next page)

Have students look at the next activity, *What's Possible?*

Part I is review, because the fact that the sum of the angles of a triangle is equal to 180° was brought out in the first unit, *Patterns*. Nevertheless, many students will benefit from a reminder of this principle, and the experience of "discovering" it in this activity will reinforce the idea.

In Part II, we want students to reach the conclusion that the sum of the lengths of any two sides must be more than the length of the third side. This fact is intimately related to *POW 18: Trying Triangles,* which will be assigned on Day 14. (This relationship between side lengths may have come up in the discussion of *Homework 12: Very Special Triangles.*)

Allow students to spend the rest of the class period on this. As they work, circulate among the groups to see that they are able to make sense of the hints for experimentation.

For any given set of numbers (either angles or sides), they should at least be able to determine if making a triangle with those numbers as side lengths or angles is possible. Drawing general conclusions from the individual experiments is harder. In the case of sides, ask them if they can see why a particular set of three numbers doesn't work—that should get them thinking in the right direction.

Parts III and IV are intended for groups that finish sooner. Students may remember or may be able to reconstruct the general angle sum formula. In terms of sides, they may come up with something similar to the triangle inequality: the longest side must be less than the sum of the other sides.

Groups will have a brief amount of time tomorrow to prepare summaries of the activity, and each group can present a part of its summary to the class.

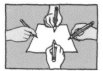

What's Possible?

This activity starts with triangles and has two initial parts—one on angles and one on sides. Parts III and IV ask about generalizations to other polygons.

Work with your group. Play around with scissors, straws, paper, protractors, and pencils. If you think other materials might help, ask if they are available.

Tomorrow, your group will give a presentation on part or on all of this activity. Chart paper will help with your presentation.

Part I: Angles

Can any three angles be the angles of a triangle?

Experiment to find the answer to this question. Start with three angles, say 30°, 50°, and 80°. Can you draw a triangle whose angles are these sizes?

Try three other values, say 50°, 60°, and 70°. Keep making up numbers and trying them. Keep track of which sets of angles are possible and which are not. What conclusions can you reach about the three angles of a triangle?

Note: You may believe that you already know the answer to the question for Part I. If so, then state what you know and how you know it.

Continued on next page

Part II: Sides

Can any three numbers be the lengths of the sides of a triangle?

Experiment to find the answer to this question. Start with three numbers, say 2, 3, and 4. Can you draw a triangle whose sides are these lengths? (You have to choose a unit of length.)

Try three other values, say 3, 6, and 11. Keep making up numbers and trying them. Keep track of which sets of lengths are possible and which are not. What conclusions can you reach about the three sides of a triangle?

Part III: Quadrilaterals

What if you were considering quadrilaterals (four-sided polygons) instead of triangles? What would be possible for the angles of a quadrilateral? What would be possible for the sides of a quadrilateral? Find conditions for quadrilaterals that are similar to those you found in Parts I and II for triangles.

Part IV: Other Polygons

How can you generalize your observations to apply to all polygons?

Homework 12   Very Special Triangles

You saw in *Why Are Triangles Special?* that triangles are special within the category of polygons.

Some triangles are even more special than others.

You've already met the *isosceles* and *equilateral* triangles, which require either two or all three of the sides to be equal. (An equilateral triangle is a special type of isosceles triangle.)

Another special category of triangle is the **right triangle**, which is a triangle with one right angle.

1. Why must the other two angles of a right triangle be acute (that is, less than 90°)?

2. Why do you think right triangles are considered important?

Continued on next page

Interactive Mathematics Program   433

Homework 12:
Very Special
Triangles

This assignment introduces some basic terminology about right triangles that will be needed later in the unit when trigonometric functions are introduced. The

• •

Triangle *ABC* shown here is a right triangle with a right angle at vertex *C*. (The small square inside that vertex is a standard symbol indicating a right angle.)

There are special names for the sides of a right triangle.

The two sides of the triangle that form the right angle, $\overline{AC}$ and $\overline{BC}$, are called the **legs** of the triangle, and the third side, $\overline{AB}$, is called the **hypotenuse**.

Note: The notation $\overline{AC}$ as used here (with a line above the letters) indicates the **line segment** from *A* to *C*. The notation *AC* (with neither the line above the letters nor the word *segment*) means the **length** of this segment. The **line** through *A* and *C* is represented by the notation $\overleftrightarrow{AC}$, and the **ray** from *A* through *C* is written $\overrightarrow{AC}$.

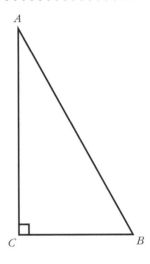

3. What statements can you make about how the lengths of the sides of a right triangle compare to each other? Explain your reasoning.

4. Draw a right triangle, measure the legs, and then draw a right triangle whose legs are twice as long.

    a. How does the hypotenuse of the new triangle compare to the hypotenuse of the original?

    b. How do the acute angles of the new triangle compare to the acute angles of the original?

    c. What do your answers to Questions 4a and 4b tell you about the two triangles?

Each of the acute angles of a right triangle is formed by the hypotenuse and one of the legs. For example, angle *A* is formed by the hypotenuse, $\overline{AB}$, and by the leg $\overline{AC}$. The leg that helps form an acute angle is said to be **adjacent to** that angle. For example, $\overline{AC}$ is the leg (or side) *adjacent to* angle *A*.

That same leg is said to be **opposite** the other acute angle. For example, $\overline{AC}$ is the leg *opposite* angle *B*.

5. Draw a right triangle in which the acute angles are different sizes. Is the longer leg *opposite* or *adjacent to* the larger of the acute angles? Do you think this is true for all right triangles?

6. Is it possible for a right triangle to be isosceles? Equilateral? Explain your answers.

434

Interactive Mathematics Program

introduction of these functions will be easier if students are already familiar with this terminology, so you should try to use the terms whenever possible.

More with Possible Triangles

Students continue to investigate the properties of triangles.

Mathematical Topics

- Working with right triangles and their terminology
- Continued work with angle sums, the triangle inequality, and generalizations of the triangle inequality

Outline of the Day

In Class

1. Select presenters for tomorrow's discussion of *POW 17: Cutting the Pie*

2. Discuss *Homework 12: Very Special Triangles*
   - Focus on getting students used to the terminology for right triangles

3. Discuss *What's Possible?* (from Day 12)
   - Review (and post, if needed) the angle sum property for triangles

   - Establish, name, and post the triangle inequality

4. Use the angle sum property for triangles to establish that two triangles with two pairs of corresponding angles equal must be similar
   - Post this principle

At Home

Homework 13: Inventing Rules

Discuss With Your Colleagues

When Will They Get the Algebra?

Students spend time in this unit solving proportion equations that would traditionally be part of an algebra course. They are mostly working on an intuitive level, rather than learning formal rules for manipulating variables (such as cross-multiplication).

Do you think they are losing out by not getting these rules now? Are they upset by the fact that students in a traditional program know some things that they don't? Are they aware that those students don't learn anything about probability, similarity, or curve-fitting in their first year of high school mathematics?

Discuss how the integration and reorganization of topics and the introduction of new content (such as probability) into the high school curriculum affect the perceptions and expectations of students, parents, and teachers.

1. POW Presentation Preparation

Presentations of *POW 17: Cutting the Pie* are scheduled for tomorrow. Choose three students to make POW presentations, and give them overhead transparencies and pens to take home to use in their preparations.

2. Discussion of Homework 12: Very Special Triangles

The primary purpose of this assignment is to introduce the terminology related to right triangles.	But the individual questions offer opportunities to build on important ideas.

You can have individual volunteers report on each question.

• Question 1

Students may have a variety of explanations as to why the other angles must be acute. You can use this opportunity to review the experimental observation made in *Patterns* that the sum of the angles of a triangle seems to be 180°. (You may want to mention to students that they will prove this fact later in this unit.)

• Question 2

The importance of right triangles will come up again during the unit, so you may want to take some time on Question 2. On the other hand, as the unit progresses, students will see the importance of right triangles through the various examples they work with. So use your judgment.

• Question 3

Students will presumably see that the hypotenuse is the longest of the three sides. The idea of the triangle inequality will come up in connection with tomorrow's activity, *What's Possible?*, so if students don't see it here, you need not bring it up yourself.

It is *not* the intent of this question to bring out the Pythagorean theorem. That important result is discussed in the Year 2 unit, *Do Bees Build It Best?*

"Does knowing the lengths of the legs of a right triangle tell you anything about the length of the hypotenuse?"

However, you may want to use the discussion of either Question 3 or Question 4 to hint at the idea that the length of the hypotenuse is *determined by* the lengths of the two legs. Students will probably not know what the nature of the relationship is, but may be able to see that there should be some function of the form $H = f(L_1, L_2)$, where H is the length of the hypotenuse and L_1 and L_2 are the lengths of the two legs.

• Question 4

Presumably students will see that the ratio of hypotenuse lengths is also 2, and that the corresponding angles are equal; that is, that the two triangles fit all the conditions for similarity.

You can summarize this into another general principle for similarity:

If the legs of two right triangles are proportional, then the triangles must be similar.

You can tell students that, later in today's work, they will look at whether just having corresponding angles equal also guarantees similarity (as they tentatively concluded in *Homework 9: Triangular Counterexamples*).

• Question 5

This question is mainly a tool for using the terms *opposite* and *adjacent*. Students will probably have no problem with the principle that the longer leg is opposite the larger angle. But it should be interesting to see what sort of explanations they can give for this phenomenon.

"Is the longest side opposite the largest angle in every triangle?"

You might ask the class if they think that the longest side is opposite the largest angle in *every* triangle. (It is.)

• Question 6

This is another look at the angle sum issue. Students should be able to figure out that a 45°-45°-90° triangle is both isosceles and right, and that there cannot be an equilateral right triangle.

• *Perpendicularity*

"What do we call two lines that meet at right angles?"

The discussion of right triangles provides a good context to introduce (or review, for some students) the word **perpendicular**. You can simply ask what we call two lines that meet at right angles.

Introduce the symbol ⊥ for perpendicularity. For example, tell students that one can express the fact that lines $\overleftrightarrow{AC}$ and $\overleftrightarrow{BC}$ in the homework diagram are perpendicular by writing $\overleftrightarrow{AC} \perp \overleftrightarrow{BC}$.

• *Acute and obtuse triangles*

"What other kinds of angles are there besides right angles?"

This is also a good opportunity to introduce terms for other types of triangles. You can start by asking what we call angles that aren't right angles. As needed, review the terms **acute angle** and **obtuse angle** (introduced in *Patterns*).

Tell students that a triangle that has an obtuse angle is called an **obtuse triangle** and that a triangle whose angles are all acute is called an **acute triangle**.

Bring out that every triangle has at least two acute angles, but that being an acute triangle requires having *all* angles acute.

3. Discussion of *What's Possible?*

You can give students about 10 minutes to finish preparing their chart-paper reports and then have the club card student report for the group. Depending on the number of groups you have, one or two groups can make presentations on each part of Questions 1 and 2.

If no one comes up with the expected conclusions, you might make a list of "Possible Sets of Angles (or Sides)" and "Impossible Sets of Angles (or Sides)," as a way of clarifying the problem. Stick with this process until they see what's going on (for triangles).

Concerning angles, students should conclude:

The sum of the angles of any triangle must be 180°.

"Have you proved this statement?"

Post this observation, perhaps labeling it the **angle sum property for triangles** for easy later reference. (It may still be posted from *Patterns*.) Point out to students that, for now, this is still an experimental observation. You can tell them that, in a few days, they will develop a proof of this fact (see the activity *A Parallel Proof* on Day 16).

Concerning sides, students should conclude:

The sum of the lengths of any two sides of a triangle must be more than the length of the third.

Tell students that this fact is called the **triangle inequality**.

Many students may benefit from seeing this condition expressed symbolically, along with an appropriately labeled diagram, as below.

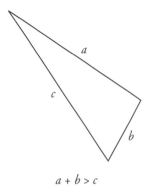

$$a + b > c$$

Some students may point out that to check if three lengths are possible sides for a triangle, you only need to verify that the two shorter ones add up to more than the longest one. In other words, you don't have to check all possible pairs of the three sides. You might point this out yourself if students don't bring it up.

"Did you find any generalization for quadrilaterals or other polygons?"

Ask if any groups have any generalizations for quadrilaterals or general polygons. If no one does, you can let it go for now, since the angle sum problem will recur shortly (see *A Parallel Proof* on Day 16).

4. Two Angles for Similarity

Ask students what the angle sum property tells them about similarity. As a hint, you can remind them that they know this fact:

If the three angles of one triangle are equal to the three angles of another triangle, then the triangles must be similar.

As an additional hint: "Everyone draw a triangle with angles of 50° and 70°, and measure the third angle."

If an additional hint is needed, you can give the class two angles, such as 50° and 70°, and have all the students draw triangles using these two angles, and perhaps measure the third angle. They should see that the resulting triangles are all similar and have the same third angle.

"How could that third angle have been found without drawing the triangle?"

If it seems needed, have someone explain how that third angle could have been found without drawing the triangles, based on the angle sum property.

Post one more general principle about similarity.

If two of the angles of one triangle are equal to two of the angles of another triangle, then the triangles must be similar.

• *Optional: What about two sides?*

Students may suggest that if it's possible to reduce the angle requirement for similarity from three angles to two, perhaps it's possible to demonstrate similarity using only two pairs of corresponding sides as well.

If they don't suggest this, you might want to pose this question:

"If two triangles have two pairs of corresponding sides proportional, do the triangles have to be similar?"

> *If two triangles have two pairs of corresponding sides proportional, do the triangles have to be similar?*

Put another way: If triangle I has sides of lengths *a*, *b*, and *c*, and triangle II has sides of lengths *d*, *e*, and *f*, with, say, $\frac{a}{d} = \frac{b}{e}$, does that guarantee similarity of the two triangles?

You can let students play with this idea until they see that the answer is no.

Homework 13: Inventing Rule
(see facing page)

This assignment will get students focused on what they actually do when they solve equations. It is preparatory for work in the second year (in the unit *Solve It!*) on solving equations by using traditional algebraic methods.

Homework 13 Inventing Rules

In working with similar triangles, you often have to solve equations involving proportions.

For example, suppose one triangle has sides of lengths 6, 9, and 14, and there is a similar triangle whose shortest side has length 15. If you use x to represent the longest side of the second triangle, then the value of x has to satisfy an equation like

$$\frac{6}{15} = \frac{14}{x}$$

(This is one of several possible equations for x.)

Continued on next page

Some such equations are easier to solve than others. Sometimes the particular numbers involved suggest tricks or shortcuts that make them easy to solve.

In each of the equations below, the letter x stands for an unknown number. Use any method you like to find the number x stands for, but write down *exactly how you do it.*

Be sure to check your answers and write down in detail how you find them.

1. $\dfrac{x}{5} = 7$ 2. $\dfrac{x}{6} = \dfrac{72}{24}$ 3. $\dfrac{x}{8} = \dfrac{11}{4}$ 4. $\dfrac{x}{7} = \dfrac{5}{3}$

5. $\dfrac{x+1}{3} = \dfrac{4}{6}$ 6. $\dfrac{5}{13} = \dfrac{19}{x}$ 7. $\dfrac{2}{x} = 6$ 8. $\dfrac{9}{x} = \dfrac{x}{16}$

POW 17
Presentations

Students present POW 17 and discuss ways to solve proportions.

Mathematical Topics

- Analyzing the numerical pattern in a geometry problem and explaining the pattern in terms of the geometry
- Optional: Summing an arithmetic sequence
- Optional: Introducing the concept of a recursive function
- Exploring ideas for solving proportions

Outline of the Day

In Class

1. Form new random groups
2. Presentations of *POW 17: Cutting the Pie*
   - Optional: Introduce language and notation of recursive functions
3. Discuss *Homework 13: Inventing Rules*
   - Have students articulate their own ideas about solving proportion equations

At Home

Homework 14: What's the Angle?

POW 18: Trying Triangles (due Day 19)

1. Forming New Groups

This is an excellent time to place the students in new random groups. Follow the procedure described in the IMP *Teaching Handbook*, and record the groups and the suit for each student.

2. Presentations of POW 17: *Cutting the Pie*

Have the three presenters give their presentations.

> It is more important that students be able to describe the pattern in the In-Out table than that they develop a closed formula. (See the supplemental problem, *Diagonals Illuminated,* in *Patterns* for a brief discussion of what is meant by a closed formula.)

"How many new pieces does the nth cut make?"

Students will probably see from the table that the nth output in the table is n more than the previous output. It may help students to think of the difference from one entry to the next as the number of *new pieces* created by the nth cut. Therefore, the total number of *new pieces* created by all n cuts is $1 + 2 + \ldots + n$. Since there is one piece (the whole pie) before any cuts are made, the nth entry in the table is $1 + (1 + 2 + \ldots + n)$.

Students may have some insights or previous experience with the sum $1 + 2 + \ldots + n,$ which will allow them to develop a closed formula for it, that is, to develop a formula without " $\ldots$ " or summation notation. However, if no student comes up with a formula, you can leave this an open question. *Note:* There is a supplemental problem in *Patterns,* called *From One to N,* that asks students to investigate this sum.

"Why does the nth cut make a maximum of n new pieces?"

You may want to ask students what ideas they have about *why* the nth cut can create a maximum of n new pieces.

> - *Optional: Recursive formula notation*
>
>   You may want to suggest the notation and symbolism of using something like a_n to represent the maximum number of pieces for n cuts. Ask the class if they can describe the rule for the table using this notation.
>
>   To be more concrete, you can start by asking how to use this notation to express a_{100}. It may help to get students to state in words how they found the 100th entry of the table, and then move toward the equation $a_{100} = a_{99} + 100$.
>
>   Once they get this, they should then be able come up with the general equation $a_n = a_{n-1} + n$, or something equivalent.
>
>   You can tell them that a formula like this is called a **recursive formula**. (The concept of a recursive formula is also discussed in the supplemental problem *Diagonals Illuminated* from *Patterns.*) You may want to point out that a recursive formula needs a "starting place," which in this problem would probably be $a_1 = 2$ or perhaps $a_0 = 1$.

3. Discussion of Homework 13: Inventing Rules

You might assign one problem to each group for presentation. Instruct the groups to compare strategies among their members and decide which method the rest of the class will understand the best. When groups appear to be ready, have the diamond card member present for the group.

Don't expect anything fancy by way of explanation, although students may come up with interesting ideas. Here are some samples of what you might hope for.

- On Question 1: "A fraction is like division, so this is saying $x \div 5 = 7$, and the answer is 35."

- On Question 3: "The denominator of the first fraction is twice as big as the denominator of the second fraction, so the numerator has to be twice as big also."

- On Question 5: "Because $\frac{4}{6}$ is the same as $\frac{2}{3}$, $\frac{x+1}{3}$ has to be equal to $\frac{2}{3}$. This means that $x + 1$ is 2, so $x = 1$."

- On Question 8: "The value for x has to be between 9 and 16. I tried all the numbers and 12 worked."

Question 7 may be difficult for many students, especially if their conceptual groundwork in fractions is weak. You may want to suggest a similar-looking but simpler problem such as $\frac{8}{x} = 4$ for comparison.

If cross-multiplying comes up, ask: "Why do you think that method works?"

Questions 4 and 6 will probably be the most challenging. If the method of cross-multiplying comes up, insist that students give some justification for the method. If they can't explain why it works, you can tell them that it is correct, but they should think about why it works.

- *Hints on working with cross-multiplication*

The following two methods are ideas you can use if students need help explaining cross-multiplication. We use Question 4, $\frac{x}{7} = \frac{5}{3}$, to illustrate.

- You can ask students to express each fraction using a common denominator, which in this case is 21. Thus, they should get

$$\frac{3x}{21} = \frac{35}{21}$$

Since the fractions have the same denominator, the numerators must also be equal, so $3x = 35$.

- You can suggest that students multiply both sides of the equation by the common denominator, 21, and simplify. Students should see that this also gives $3x = 35$. (The general idea of multiplying both sides of an equation to get an equivalent equation will be discussed in the Year 2 unit *Solve It!*, but it should make intuitive sense here.)

"Where did the 3x come from? Where did the 35 come from?"

In either case, help students to see that the two sides of the final equation, 3x and 35, could each have been obtained by multiplying a numerator by the "opposite" denominator.

You can also use known pairs of equivalent fractions to verify that cross-multiplying gives equal products.

You may want to get students to go through one of these methods in a more symbolic form, beginning with a general proportion, $\frac{a}{b} = \frac{c}{d}$, and using the common denominator bd to lead to the equation $ad = bc$. This general form may make it clearer where the final equation comes from.

Homework 14: What's the Angle?
(see facing page)

In tomorrow's discussion of this assignment, students will be introduced to some of the standard terminology used in referring to various related angles.

POW 18: Trying Triangles
(see page 108)

This problem is primarily about the triangle inequality, but it also involves a review of some ideas about probability.

You should provide pipe cleaners (or something similar, such as long "twisties") for students to use on this problem. You may want to give a brief demonstration of how one would make a triangle from three segments of a pipe cleaner.

Discussion of this POW is scheduled for Day 19.

Homework 14

What's the Angle?

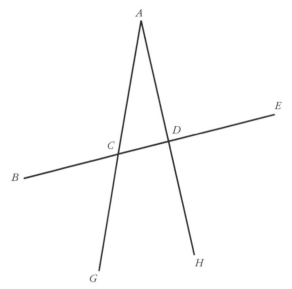

You've seen that angles play a very important role in similarity. So it's useful to know when two angles are sure to be equal.

The diagram at the right is made up of three line segments: $\overline{AG}$, $\overline{AH}$ and $\overline{BE}$

$\overline{BE}$ intersects $\overline{AG}$ at point C and intersects $\overline{AH}$ at point D.

There are also lots of angles in the diagram. Your first task in this assignment is to explore the relationships between those angles. Then test whether your observations apply to similar diagrams.

Note: Some of these angles can be described easily by a single letter, such as $\angle A$. In other cases, you need three letters to specify the angle you mean. For example, writing $\angle C$ would be ambiguous. That is, it would be unclear which angle was meant because there are several angles in the diagram that have C as the vertex. If you write $\angle ACD$, there shouldn't be any confusion. Be sure to express all your angles using notation that is clear.

You may want to use a protractor to gather some information, but you should also find explanations for *why* certain angle relationships hold. That will allow you to generalize your results.

1. Based on your exploration of the specific diagram above, answer questions like these:

   • Which angles are equal to which other angles?

   • What angle sum relationships can you find?

2. Draw some other diagrams to test whether the relationships you found in Question 1 were specific to that diagram or examples of a general principle.

3. Generalize from your work in Questions 1 and 2, and justify your general conclusions.

POW 18 *Trying Triangles*

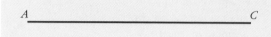

Suppose you have a straight pipe cleaner of a given length.

For convenience, label the two ends of the pipe cleaner *A* and *C*, as shown at the left.

Now suppose that the pipe cleaner is bent into two portions, with one portion twice as long as the other. Label the place where the bend is made *B*, as shown at the left, so that the segment from *B* to *C* is twice as long as the segment from *A* to *B*.

Then a fourth point, *X,* is chosen at random somewhere on the longer section, and the pipe cleaner is bent at that place as well. So now the pipe cleaner might look like the illustration below.

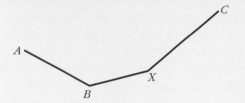

Can the three segments of the pipe cleaner be made into a triangle by changing the angles at the two bends? As you might suppose, the answer depends on the location of point *X*.

So here's the question.

> *If point X is chosen at random along the section from B to C, what is the probability that the three segments of the pipe cleaner can be made into a triangle?*

(Recall that "chosen at random" means that all positions between *B* and *C* are equally likely to be selected as the location for point *X*.)

Continued on next page

As part of your investigation of this problem, you will probably first need to come up with the answer to this question:

> *Suppose three lengths, a, b, and c, are given. What condition must these lengths satisfy for it to be possible to make a triangle whose sides have these three lengths?*

Note: You may find it helpful to assume that the original pipe cleaner has a specific length.

Write-up

1. *Problem Statement*

2. *Process*

3. *Solution:* Your solution should include answers to both questions posed above.

4. *Evaluation*

Adapted from *Mathematics Teacher* (November 1989), National Council of Teachers of Mathematics, Volume 82, Number 6.

More About Angles

Students explore some general relationships between angles, including vertical angles and angles formed by a transversal across parallel lines.

Mathematical Topics

- Supplementary angles, straight angles, and vertical angles
- Angles formed by a transversal through two parallel lines

Outline of the Day

In Class

1. Discuss *Homework 14: What's the Angle?*
   - Introduce the terms **supplementary angles** and **vertical angles**
   - Use supplementary angles to establish that vertical angles are equal

2. *More About Angles*
   - Students investigate the angles formed by a transversal through two parallel lines

3. Discuss *More About Angles*
   - Introduce the terms **corresponding angles** and **alternate interior angles**
   - Confirm students' observations about corresponding and alternate interior angles
   - Tell students about the parallel postulate

At Home

Homework 15: Inside Similarity

Discuss With Your Colleagues

The Parallel Postulate

The history surrounding Euclid's fifth postulate reflects one of the extraordinary intellectual achievements in mathematics—the pursuit of logic until it led to the creation of entirely new ways of thinking about geometry.

What is the best way to treat this history? Does it belong in a math class? In a philosophy class? In a "Great Ideas" class?

1. Discussion of *Homework 14: What's the Angle?*

Let several heart card students share some of their observations, along with explanations.

"How are angles ACD and BCG related to angle BCA?"

As examples arise, introduce the appropriate terminology. For example, someone is likely to point out that $\angle ACD = \angle BCG$. Explanations may vary, but if no one suggests it, you can ask how each of these angles is related to $\angle BCA$. Students should be able to state these relationships:

$$\angle ACD + \angle BCA = 180°$$

and

$$\angle BCG + \angle BCA = 180°$$

"If you knew, say, that angle BCA was 110°, what other angles could you find?"

As a hint, you can tell students to imagine, say, that $\angle BCA = 110°$, and ask them if they can find the size of any other angles.

"What do you call a pair of angles that add up to 180°?"

Ask if anyone knows the term for a pair of angles whose sum is 180°. If no one does, tell them that such angles are called **supplementary angles**, and each is called the **supplement** of the other.

> Be sure students realize that the term *supplementary* refers to a relationship between angles—a single angle cannot be "supplementary."

Also introduce the term **straight angle** as a synonym for an angle of 180°—that is, an angle whose two sides go in opposite directions—and point out that a pair of angles that fit together to form a straight angle are supplementary. This terminology may be useful to students in tomorrow's activity, *A Parallel Proof*.

"How can the two equations above be used to prove that ∠ACD = ∠BCG?"

Next, ask how the two equations above can be used to *prove* that $\angle ACD = \angle BCG$. Again, if a hint is needed, tell the class to suppose that they know the value of $\angle BCA$, and ask how they would find each of the other two angles in the equations. They should see that they have two equations

As a hint:
"If you know angle BCA, how can you find angles ACD and BCG?"

$$\angle ACD = 180° - \angle BCA$$

and

$$\angle BCG = 180° - \angle BCA$$

Taken together, these equations show that the angles are equal.

Introduce the term **vertical angles** for a pair of "opposite" angles formed by the intersection of two lines, such as angles *ACD* and *BCG*. (As with the term *supplementary,* be sure students realize that the term *vertical* refers to a relationship *between* angles.)

"What relationship holds for vertical angles?"

Ask if anyone can state a general principle about such angles. They should be able to see that this statement holds true:

Vertical angles are always equal.

You may also want to introduce the following observation, which is essentially the proof of the statement above.

Angles that are supplements of the same angle must be equal.

In addition to noticing the equality of the vertical angles and seeing the angle sums for the adjacent supplementary angles, someone may also mention that the angles of triangle *ACD* add up to 180°.

If this doesn't come up, that's fine, but if it does, you can use the occasion to point out again that, so far, this angle sum is only a measurement observation, while the other relationships stated above are proven certainties. You can tell students that tomorrow they will see a proof of the angle sum property, using ideas from this homework discussion.

2. *More About Angles*
(see next page)

This activity continues the process of developing student insight into angle relationships.

3. Discussion of *More About Angles*

Let several spade card students share their observations about the angles in the diagram.

They should see, for example, that angles *ACD* and *CFG* are equal and that angles *BCF* and *CFG* are equal.

Tell students that there is standard terminology for referring to certain pairs of angles in a diagram like this one.

More About Angles

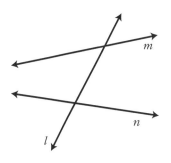

In this activity, you will continue your investigation of the angles formed when lines intersect.

In general, a line that intersects two or more other lines is called a **transversal** for those other lines.

For example, in the diagram at the left, the line labeled *l* is a transversal for the pair of lines labeled *m* and *n*.

The case where the two lines *m* and *n* are parallel is especially important, and that's the subject of this activity.

In the second diagram at the left, $\overleftrightarrow{BD}$ and $\overleftrightarrow{EG}$ are parallel lines. $\overleftrightarrow{AH}$ is a transversal that intersects $\overleftrightarrow{BD}$ at C and intersects $\overleftrightarrow{EG}$ at F.

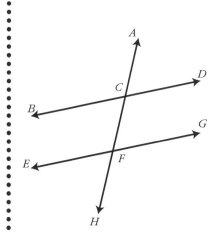

Investigate the angles in this diagram, focusing on these two questions:

- Which angles are equal to which other angles?

- What angle sum relationships can you find?

Pay special attention to the angle relationships that occur because $\overleftrightarrow{BD}$ and $\overleftrightarrow{EG}$ are parallel.

---

440   Interactive Mathematics Program

"Angles ACD and CFG are called corresponding angles. What other pairs do you think are called corresponding angles?"

You might introduce this terminology by identifying a pair of angles, such as *ACD* and *CFG,* as **corresponding angles**, and asking the class to find other pairs that they think form corresponding angles.

"Why do suppose these angles are called corresponding angles?"

It will be helpful to many students if you use the diagram to bring out why these angles are called "corresponding." For example, angles *ACD* and *CFG* (labeled 1 and 2 below for clarity) are each "above and to the right" of their vertices, *C* and *F*.

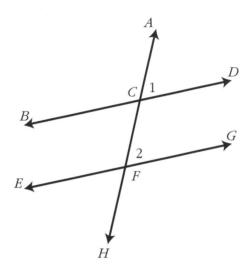

"Why do suppose these angles are called alternate interior angles?"

You can then introduce the term **alternate interior angles**, perhaps using the pair of angles *BCF* and *CFG.* A diagram will again be helpful in explaining the name. You can describe the area between the parallel lines as the *interior* of the diagram and point out that angles *BCF* and *CFG* (angles 3 and 2 below) are both in this interior region and are on "alternate" sides of the transversal.

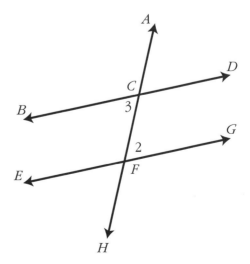

Try to get students to develop general statements like these:

When a transversal cuts across parallel lines, the corresponding angles are equal.

and

When a transversal cuts across parallel lines, the alternate interior angles are equal.

You might also bring out the connection between these two statements, using the idea of vertical angles. For instance, if angles *ACD* and *CFG* are equal, then angles *BCF* and *CFG* must also be equal, since angles *ACD* and *BCF* are vertical angles.

• *Why are these angles equal?*

"How do you know that corresponding angles or alternate interior angles are equal?"

At some point, ask students how they know that corresponding angles or alternate interior angles are equal. One likely response is for them to say that they measured the angles, and they came out the same.

"Can you explain it in a way that uses the fact that the lines are parallel?"

You should push for something more intrinsic to the situation, that is, an explanation that uses the parallelism of the lines. (It's probably easier to work with corresponding angles, and then deduce the principle for alternate interior angles by the reasoning just described.)

For example, a student might say, "Angles *ACD* and *CFG* are equal because the lines forming the angles are facing the same way." Or they might describe something like "sliding angle *AFG* along line *AH* until *F* reaches point *C*." In any case, trying to verbalize why those angles are equal will strengthen their intuition.

• *Optional: An axiom on parallel lines*

Tell students that in formal work with geometry, some fundamental assumption must be made about parallel lines, and then other principles are proved on the basis of that fundamental assumption. You can tell students that such a fundamental assumption is called an **axiom** or a **postulate**.

Some traditional high school geometry textbooks take as an axiom that corresponding angles formed by a transversal across parallel lines must be equal.

You can tell students that modern formal geometry usually assumes the following principle, known as the **parallel postulate**:

Given any line *L* and any point *P* not on line *L*, there is a unique line through *P* that is parallel to *L*.

You may want to mention that proving the principles on corresponding and alternate interior angles from the parallel postulate is not trivial. (The proof is indirect and uses the fact that an exterior angle of a triangle must be greater than either of the nonadjacent interior angles.)

Note: There is a supplemental problem, *The Parallel Postulate,* in which students are to research and report on the history of the parallel postulate and its role in non-Euclidean geometry.

Homework 15:
Inside Similarity
(see next page)

In this homework, students will learn how to form similar triangles within each other. Knowing how to do this will be helpful in one approach to solving the *Shadows* unit problem and should also deepen students' understanding of similarity.

Homework 15   Inside Similarity

How do you make small triangles inside larger ones so that the small ones are similar to the large ones?

The diagram below shows two triangles that are congruent to the top triangle. In each case, a dotted line has been drawn that connects two sides of the triangle and cuts off a smaller (shaded) triangle.

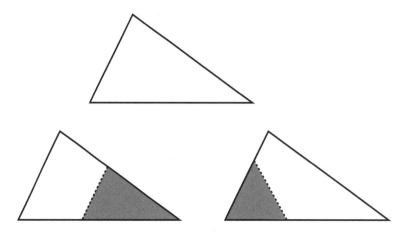

In the first case, the smaller triangle appears to be similar to the larger one. In the second case, the smaller triangle seems not to be similar to the larger one.

Your task is to investigate and report on the difference between these two cases. That is, if you connect points on two sides of a triangle, when does the smaller triangle created in this way come out similar to the original?

You may want to begin your investigation by tracing the original triangle and experimenting by drawing some lines on your tracing. Find as many ways as you can to draw lines to cut off small triangles that are similar to the original triangle.

Then describe in words those lines that can be used to cut off a small triangle that is similar to the larger one, and explain your answer.

DAY 16 *A Parallel Proof*

Students use parallel lines to prove that the sum of the angles of a triangle is 180°.

Mathematical Topics

- Seeing that a line parallel to a side of a triangle creates a similar triangle
- Proving—using parallel lines—that the sum of the angles of a triangle is 180°
- Further insight into the angle sum formula for polygons

• •

Outline of the Day

In Class

1. Discuss *Homework 15: Inside Similarity*
   - Use corresponding angles to establish that a line parallel to a side of a triangle creates a similar triangle
2. *A Parallel Proof*
   - Students develop a proof of the angle sum property for triangles

3. Discuss *A Parallel Proof*
   - Emphasize that the proof is based on an assumption about angles formed from parallel lines

At Home

Homework 16: Ins and Outs of Proportion

Note: Tomorrow and the next day you will need mirrors in class. You will probably be able to get enough by asking students today to bring them in. (No particular size is needed.) You will only need one mirror per group (or one per pair if you wish).

Also, you will want to be able to darken your classroom tomorrow for the activity *Bouncing Light*.

1. Discussion of *Homework 15: Inside Similarity*

Ask students to work in their groups to compile a list of ways to form a similar small triangle. Tell them you will ask the club card student from each group to report. Then ask groups to report.

Students should have seen that a line through the triangle parallel to any side will give a similar small triangle.

The dotted lines in the diagrams below illustrate the three families of lines that fit this description:

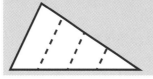 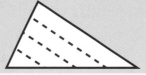 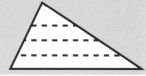

"Why does a line parallel to one side make a similar triangle?"

Ask students to try to explain why a line parallel to one side makes a similar triangle. They should see that the large and small triangles share one angle, and that the corresponding angles formed by the parallel lines are equal, so the triangles have equal angles.

Note: Lines parallel to a side of the triangle are not the only lines that create similar triangles. For example, the diagram below shows a shaded triangle that is formed by drawing a line parallel to the base. Angles x and y are marked to help keep track of what happens.

The shaded triangle can now be rotated and placed back inside the original triangle, as shown in the next diagram. Notice that angle y of the small triangle still fits in the same place in the original triangle, even though the small triangle has been flipped and rotated.

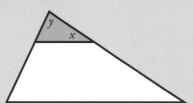 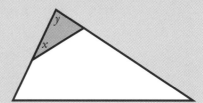

Now suppose this shaded triangle is flipped, as shown in the next diagram.

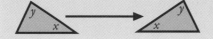

Here, the shaded triangle is still similar to the original large triangle, but the line creating this shaded triangle is not parallel to any of the sides of the original triangle.

2. *A Parallel Proof*

(see next page)

Building on yesterday's activity, *More About Angles,* students should be ready to create one of the traditional proofs of the angle sum property for triangles.

Let them work in their groups on *A Parallel Proof.* If a hint seems needed, you can ask what angles must be equal and what angle sum is easy to find.

3. Discussion of *A Parallel Proof*

After most groups seem to have found the proof, you can have one or two presentations of the reasoning.

There are basically three steps to the argument.

- $x = s$ and $y = t$, since these are pairs of alternate interior angles formed by a transversal across parallel lines.

- $x + r + y = 180°$, since these angles form a straight angle; that is, they add up to half of a complete turn.

- Substitution of s for x and t for y gives $s + r + t = 180°$, as desired.

Since the angle sum formula for triangles has been dangling since Day 19 of the *Patterns* unit, you may want to have some fanfare about finally proving it.

Note: An alternate proof, based on the use of exterior angles, is the central point in the somewhat lengthy supplemental problem, *Exterior Angles and Polygon Angle Sums.*

- *Optional: What's assumed?*

You may want to point out that the above proof of the angle sum formula is based on the alternate interior angle principle. You can ask students how they know that the alternate interior angle principle is exact or always true.

One might justify the principle by measurement, but then it doesn't make sense to make a big deal out of the proof of the angle sum formula, since that formula can be justified on its own by measurement.

One might then point out that one can prove the alternate interior angle principle from the corresponding angles principle, but then one needs to justify the corresponding angles principle.

In other words, every attempt to justify one of these principles seems to rest on another, experimentally based principle.

If you want to resolve this issue with students, you will need to tell them that, ultimately, one of these principles must be taken on faith or used as a fundamental assumption. As noted yesterday, such an assumption is called an *axiom* or *postulate.*

A Parallel Proof

For some time, you've known from measurement that the sum of the angles of any triangle seems to be 180°. Now it's time to see why this must be true.

In this activity, you will be given a diagram involving an arbitrary triangle. Your task will be to show how to use this diagram to prove the angle sum property for triangles.

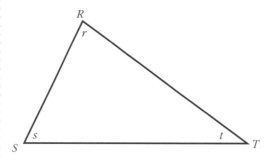

To get started, suppose *RST* is any triangle, such as the one shown at the left.

For convenience, the angles of this triangle are labeled *r*, *s*, and *t*.

Next, draw a line through vertex *R* that is parallel to the opposite side. This is the line $\overleftrightarrow{AB}$ shown in the diagram below, in which $\overleftrightarrow{AB}$ is parallel to $\overleftrightarrow{ST}$. The angles *ARS* and *BRT* have been labeled *x* and *y* in this new diagram.

Your task is to show how this diagram can be used to prove the angle sum property for triangles. In other words, prove that the angles labeled *r*, *s*, and *t* add up to 180°.

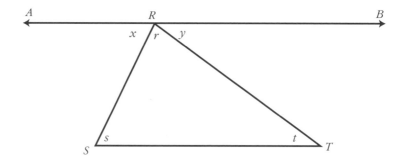

Continued on next page

You can tell students that one might take the angle sum formula itself as an axiom, but that mathematicians prefer to use something that is more "intuitively obvious" as an axiom. Most mathematicians feel that the principle on corresponding angles is more "obvious" than the angle sum formula (see the intuitive explanations of this principle in the Day 15 subsection "Why are these angles equal?"), and so they consider it worthwhile to prove the angle sum formula from this other principle.

Hint: You may find it helpful to extend the sides of the original triangle, as shown below. In this diagram, both $\overleftrightarrow{EF}$ and $\overleftrightarrow{GH}$ are transversals for the parallel lines $\overleftrightarrow{AB}$ and $\overleftrightarrow{CD}$. Think about how to use the transversals to get information about angles.

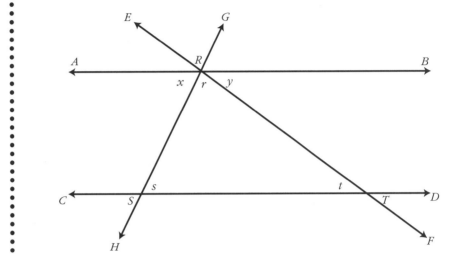

Homework 16

Ins and Outs of Proportion

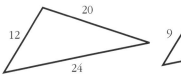

Triangle 1   Triangle 2

The two triangles above are similar, since the ratios between a side of Triangle 1 and the corresponding side of Triangle 2 are the same for all three sides.

In other words, the three ratios $\frac{12}{9}$, $\frac{20}{15}$, and $\frac{24}{18}$ are equal. For triangles, having corresponding sides proportional guarantees similarity.

What about ratios of sides *within* a triangle? For example, the ratio of the longest to the shortest side in Triangle 1 is $\frac{24}{12}$, while the corresponding ratio in Triangle 2 is $\frac{18}{9}$. These two ratios are also equal, since both fractions are equal to 2.

1. Compare the other ratios within each triangle. In other words, find a different ratio of two sides of Triangle 1, and find the corresponding ratio in Triangle 2, and compare. Do this for all possible pairs of sides.

   What do you conclude?

2. Form another pair of similar triangles. (To get corresponding sides in proportion, you can use any convenient set of lengths for the sides of the first triangle, and multiply those numbers by a fixed value to get the lengths of the sides of the second triangle.)

   Now repeat Question 1 for your new pair of triangles. That is, find the ratio of a pair of sides of your first new triangle, find the corresponding ratio in your second new triangle, and compare.

3. Form a third pair of triangles, but this time make them not similar. Examine the ratios of sides within one triangle to the ratios of sides within the other. What do you conclude?

Continued on next page

Homework 16:
Ins and Outs of
Proportion

This homework raises an issue that may have come up earlier, but which will be important in the discussion of trigonometric ratios later in the unit.

4. Now consider the two triangles at the right. Assume that they are similar, so the ratios $\frac{r}{x}$, $\frac{s}{y}$, and $\frac{t}{z}$ are all equal.

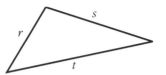

Triangle 3

a. Based on your results in Questions 1 through 3, identify a pair of ratios—one using sides of Triangle 3 and one using sides of Triangle 4—that you think are equal to each other.

b. Find as many pairs of equal ratios as you can.

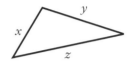

Triangle 4

Days
17-20

Lights and Shadows

You know that shadows have something to do with light (or lack of it). You're almost ready to solve the lamp shadow problem, but first you will look at some fascinating situations that involve light in a different context. Similar triangles continue to be the main theme.

This page in the student book introduces Days 17 through 20.

Lydia Gracia measures Michelle France's shadow to compare it to the shadow of a light pole.

446

Interactive Mathematics Program

DAY 17 Bouncing Light

Students explore what happens when light bounces off a mirror.

Mathematical Topics

- Seeing two types of proportions for the sides of similar triangles
- Using mirrors and similar triangles for indirect measurement
- Discovering experimentally that the angle of approach equals the angle of departure

Outline of the Day

In Class

1. Discuss *Homework 16: Ins and Outs of Proportion*
   - Identify two principles of proportion for two similar triangles:
     - ✓ the ratio between any pair of sides in the first triangle is equal to the ratio between the corresponding pair of sides within the second triangle
     - ✓ the ratio between a side of the first triangle and the corresponding side of the second triangle is the same no matter which side of the first triangle you use

2. *Bouncing Light*
   - Students investigate the reflection of light off a mirror

3. Discuss *Bouncing Light*
   - State and post the principle that the angle of approach is equal to the angle of departure

At Home

Homework 17: Now You See It, Now You Don't

Special Materials Needed

- Flashlights—one per group
- Masking tape (to narrow the flashlights' beams)
- A mirror for each group or each pair

Discuss With Your Colleagues

Why Not Solve the Problem?

By this point in the unit, students have the tools to solve the unit problem, yet they aren't asked to do so until Day 21. Discuss what is achieved by interposing several days of additional activities about measurement.

1. Discussion of *Homework 16: Ins and Outs of Proportion*

You can begin by letting two or three students share their general conclusions or results on Question 4. They should have seen that if two triangles are similar, then a ratio of sides within one triangle is equal to the ratio of the corresponding sides in the second triangle.

In other words, the assumption of similarity—that is, that the ratios $\frac{r}{x}$, $\frac{s}{y}$, and $\frac{t}{z}$ are equal—leads, for example, to the conclusion that the ratios $\frac{r}{s}$ and $\frac{x}{y}$ are equal.

Build as much as possible on students' earlier work with the algebra of proportions to bring out the connection between the geometric and algebraic perspectives in this situation.

In particular, you can talk about the idea that a triangle of a given shape has a characteristic 3-step ratio of its sides, and any similar triangle has the same ratio.

For example, if one triangle has sides of lengths 5, 7, and 9, then the sides of any similar triangle must be in the ratio 5 : 7 : 9. *Note:* We usually use the word *ratio* for only two numbers, but it can also be used in this way.

Comment: Our own familiarity with the algebra of manipulating proportions may make us overlook the geometrical distinction between the two types of ratios considered in this homework. But students will have learned about similarity in terms of the equality of ratios formed by comparing a side of one polygon to the corresponding side of another. They may not automatically make the transition to the equality of corresponding ratios *within* polygons.

Ins and Outs of Proportions is included at this point of the unit partly in order to set the stage for the study of ratios *within right triangles*, which is the basic idea of trigonometry. These ratios will be introduced in *Homework 22: Right Triangle Ratios* and formalized as trigonometric functions on Day 23.

2. *Bouncing Light*
(see page 130)

Have students turn to the activity *Bouncing Light*. Tell them that they will be doing an experiment that will tie into new ways of measuring things by using similar triangles. This would be a good experiment to do in twos or threes. But if you don't have enough flashlights or mirrors, let students work in their usual groups (or combine groups, if needed).

Since the flashlight's beam of light is more easily seen against a plain background, you may want to hand out chart paper and suggest that groups tape the paper onto the desk. That way they can trace the path of light directly onto the chart paper.

You may need to partially darken the room for this activity. It will also help to put masking tape on the flashlight lens so that only a sliver of light will pass through it. By doing so, you will make the beam of light less dispersed and easier to see as a "line" bouncing off the mirror. Remind the students to mark not only the path of light, but the mirror position also.

• *Angles of Approach and Departure*

You may be used to the terms **angle of incidence** and **angle of reflection**. However, these refer formally to angles between the light and the line *perpendicular* to the mirror, not between the light and the mirror itself. Since the angles between the ray of light and the mirror itself seem more natural to work with, we have used the terms **angle of approach** and **angle of departure** to refer to these angles, as shown here. You should go over these terms with the class.

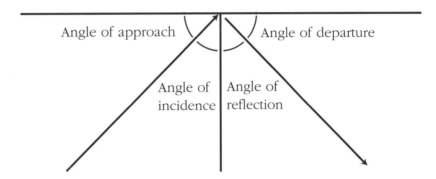

• *Possible preliminaries*

Students have many misconceptions regarding images in mirrors and the bouncing of light. For example, they may have trouble knowing where to look in the mirror to find something that's out of sight, and they may be confused at seeing directions reversed.

You may want to give groups some introductory tasks, such as placing a mirror on the ground and asking them to stand so that they can see the top of the chalkboard in the mirror. This will help them develop their intuitive sense of the way mirrors work.

You can also ask one student to hold the mirror so that another student can see an object, like a window, door, or poster, reflected in it. You can have them state aloud how they are deciding where to place the mirror and what is happening as they move it.

3. Discussion of Bouncing Light

When you believe students have had sufficient time to work with the flashlights and mirrors, bring the class together for a discussion. Discuss what the students learned. Theoretically, the two angles should be equal.

Bouncing Light

If you take a flashlight and shine it into a mirror, the light will "bounce off" the mirror. In this activity, you will look at the angles involved in such "bouncing light."

Set up your flashlight and mirror in a way similar to that shown in the sketch below.

That is, one person can hold the mirror, another can shine the flashlight at the mirror, and a third can mark the path along which the reflection of the light leaves the mirror.

The angle between the mirror and the incoming ray of light from the flashlight is called the **angle of approach**. The angle between the mirror and the ray bouncing off the mirror is called the **angle of departure**.

Continued on next page

You should post this observation in the room:

> **Principle of Light Reflection: When light is reflected off a surface, the angle of approach is equal to the angle of departure.**

1. Use a protractor to measure the angle of approach and the angle of departure. (You may want to trace the path of the flashlight's beam to and from the mirror onto chart paper.)

   What do you notice about the relationship between the two angles?

2. Repeat this experiment but change the angle at which the beam goes into the mirror. Do this two more times to see whether the relationship that you observed between the angles always seems to hold true. Write down what you've noticed about the relationship.

3. Hold the mirror in different positions to look at other things in the classroom. What do you notice about the position of the mirror? Write about the relationship between your observations in Question 2 and how you have to hold the mirror. Try to explain what looking at something in a mirror has to do with bouncing light.

Homework 17 Now You See It, Now You Don't

Use the principle of light reflection and your protractor to answer the following problems. You will need to trace each of the diagrams in this assignment.

1. A person is standing at point *A*, looking toward the mirror. Which letters of the alphabet can this person see?

A
•   *B C D E F G H I J K L M*

2. Two spiders are on opposite walls. A large mirror is placed on the floor.

   Copy the diagram below, and show exactly where on the floor the spiders should look to see each other. Can you find two triangles that are similar in your drawing? Why must they be similar?

Mirror

*Homework 17:
Now You See It,
Now You Don't*

Most students will do this homework by using an experimental approach.

DAY 18 *Mirror Magic*

Students use the principle of light reflection to measure the heights of objects.

Mathematical Topics

- Using the principle of light reflection
- Measuring heights by using similar triangles

Outline of the Day

In Class

1. Select presenters for tomorrow's discussion of *POW 18: Trying Triangles*

2. Discuss *Homework 17: Now You See It, Now You Don't*
   - Have students use similar triangles to discover where the spiders should look

3. *Mirror Magic*
   - Students use mirrors and similar triangles to measure distances indirectly

4. Discuss *Mirror Magic*
   - Focus on the use of similar triangles

At Home

Homework 18: Mirror Madness

1. POW Presentation Preparation

Presentations of *POW 18: Trying Triangles* are scheduled for tomorrow. Choose three students to make POW presentations, and give them overhead transparencies and pens to take home to use in their preparations.

2. Discussion of *Homework 17: Now You See It, Now You Don't*

You can let students compare their answers with one another in their groups for a few minutes, and then start the discussion. Question 1 should be fairly straightforward, with students connecting point *A* to each end of the mirror and drawing the reflection lines.

"How did you get your point in Question 2?"

Ask students for explanations of their result on Question 2. Watch for students who automatically use the *halfway* point for the reflection on this problem.

"What similar triangles are involved?"

"How do you know the triangles are similar?"

If necessary, ask what similar triangles are involved, and how students know that the triangles are similar. They should be able to identify the similar triangles *RST* and *VUT* in a schematic diagram like the one below, and to prove their similarity using the two-angle principle (by means of the pair of right angles and the pair of angles *RTS* and *VTU* that are equal by the principle of light reflection).

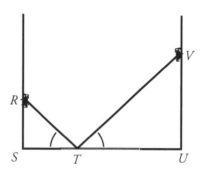

"What fraction of the way from S to U is T?"

You can also ask students to describe where point *T* should go as a fraction of the way along the segment from *S* to *U* (especially if some students thought *T* should be the midpoint of $\overline{SU}$). Try to get them to explain that, because of the similar triangles, the two lengths *ST* and *TU* should be in the same ratio as *RS* and *VU*.

3. Mirror Magic

(see page 136)

In *Mirror Magic,* students are asked to find the height of objects in the room using a mirror and a yardstick or meterstick. You can suggest that they work through a few examples where they can reach the object and confirm their measurement and work through some where they can't.

You can begin the activity by having the class read the material that precedes the questions. Next, have one or two students act out the scenario for the class. You may assign objects and have the students find the heights, or you can allow them to pick their own. If you anticipate problems in this regard, then you can tape pieces of paper with group numbers on them around the walls at differing heights.

With this introduction, have students begin work.

> In this activity, students are being given less in the way of structure or hints than in earlier problems. It is hoped that, in drawing their diagrams, they will find appropriate similar triangles. The second diagram below is a more schematic version of the first, and may make the similar triangles more apparent.
>
> In this set up, students can measure the person's height, the distance along the floor from the person to the mirror, and the distance along the floor from the mirror to the object, and then set up a proportion to find the height of the object.

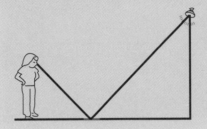
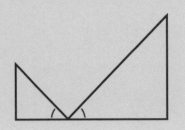

They may need some hints along the way to get them started. In particular, they might need suggestions about how to use the principle of light reflection to create the similar triangles.

As they work on this in their groups, you can make minimal hints as needed. As much as possible, let them figure out how to put the concepts together.

As students finish work in groups on the assignment, you may want to pass out overhead transparencies or chart paper for the reports. Tell them that the diamond card student will report on the group's conclusions, and give them a few minutes to work together to summarize their ideas. If some groups finish early, give them values for three of the four variables and have them solve for the fourth.

4. Discussion of *Mirror Magic*

Have diamond card students from groups that prepared reports explain what information they would need in order to calculate the height of their object and how they would use this information. Emphasize their use of diagrams.

At this stage, the focus should be on setting up the mathematics of the problem, and not on solving for the height of the object.

It is expected that students will use what they know about similar triangles to get something like the following proportion:.

$$\frac{\text{height of object}}{\text{height of person}} = \frac{\text{distance from mirror to object}}{\text{distance from mirror to person}}$$

Mirror Magic

You can actually use a mirror and the principle of light reflection to measure the heights of objects. All that is needed is a flat surface on which to place your mirror.

The method uses similar triangles, and it begins like this:

> You lay the mirror on the ground some distance from the object. Then you move slowly backwards, away from the object, while looking down at the mirror. At some point, you should be able to see the object in your mirror.

Continued on next page

The distances here are measured along the ground. (It would be mathematically correct to use the distances to the top of the object and the person, but these can't be measured easily.) Also note that *height of person* is really *height of person's eye.*

You then measure some things that are easier to measure than the height of the given object and apply ideas of geometry.

1. Find the height of an object in the classroom using this method.

2. Make a diagram that shows your method. Label the distances that you measured, and show how you used these measurements to find the height of the object.

3. Assign variables to the distances you measured, and set up an In-Out table in which these variables are labels for the input columns. Assign a variable for the height of your object and use that as the label for the output column.

   Enter your actual measurements as the first row of inputs of your table, and put the height you got as the first output.

4. Next, make up some numbers for your input variables. Then, based on your made-up numbers, find the new height of the object.

   In other words, find some more rows for your table, calculating the output (the height) in terms of the numbers you made up. The geometric situation in your diagram should serve as the basis for your calculation.

5. Give a description in words or write an equation that shows the relationship between the height of the object and your input variables.

"What variables do you want to use for these measurements?"

Students should introduce letter variables to describe the four measurements involved. If they do not, then push them in that direction. The variables should be included in the diagrams they make as well as in the discussion of equations.

If they are able to analyze the arithmetic by which they found the *height of object* numbers, they are likely to come up with a formula like this:

$$\text{height of object} = \text{height of person} \cdot \frac{\text{distance from mirror to object}}{\text{distance from mirror to person}}$$

They might not, *and need not,* see this equation as derived algebraically from the first. There may be a gap between what they understand when they are solving for x in a specific numerical equation like

$$\frac{x}{5} = \frac{20}{3}$$

and what they understand in terms of solving for x in a generic equation like

$$\frac{x}{a} = \frac{b}{c}$$

If students derive the rule for the In-Out table directly from the general equation, make sure they all see that it also explains the In-Out table.

Homework 18: Mirror Madness
(see facing page)

This homework is a playful activity about similar triangles and mirrors.

Homework 18   Mirror Madness

A family of spiders has found a bunch of mirrors on the ground, and they have been positioning themselves to see each other in the mirrors.

They are dangling in the order shown below, although their distances from each other, their heights off the ground, and the positions of the mirrors are not necessarily drawn to scale.

Sister spider, who is 48 inches off the ground, can see Momma spider in a mirror that is on the ground between them. This mirror is 20 inches from the point directly below Sister spider and 30 inches from the point directly below Momma.

Momma spider can see Uncle spider in a mirror that is 10 inches from the point below Momma and 5 inches from the point below Uncle.

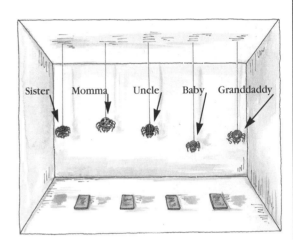

Uncle spider can see Baby spider in a mirror that is 8 inches from the point below Uncle and 6 inches from the point below Baby.

Finally, Baby spider can see Granddaddy spider in a mirror that is 12 inches from the point below Baby and 16 inches from the point below Granddaddy.

Your Assignment

Find the height of each spider. (You already know the height of Sister spider.)

Show your equations and how you solved them.

Interactive Mathematics Program

POW 18
Presentations

Mathematical Topics

- Using similar triangles and the principle of light reflection
- Using the triangle inequality in a problem context

Outline of the Day

In Class

1. Discuss *Homework 18: Mirror Madness*
2. Presentations of *POW 18: Trying Triangles*
   - Focus on the use of the triangle inequality

At Home

Homework 19: To Measure a Tree

POW 19: Pool Pockets (due Day 25)

1. Discussion of *Homework 18: Mirror Madness*

The amount of discussion needed for this assignment will probably depend on how comfortable your students were with yesterday's activity, *Mirror Magic.*

If you do spend time discussing this homework, the focus should be on the use of similarity to set up equations, rather than on techniques of solving equations. At this point, the solution of equations should be left on an intuitive level, and you should not look for mastery of techniques.

For example, to find the height of Momma spider, students might create a diagram like this:

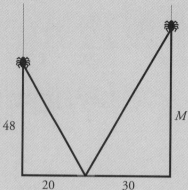

They should be able to explain why the two triangles are similar (using the principle of light reflection) and then use the similarity to set up an equation such as this:

$$\frac{20}{30} = \frac{48}{M}$$

They may then use a variety of methods, including trial and error, to find the numerical value for M that fits the equation.

2. Presentations of POW 18: *Trying Triangles*

Ask the three students to make their POW presentations. If other students have different answers or explanations, let them share their ideas.

The key idea is the triangle inequality, discussed on Day 13, according to which the longest side must be less than the sum of the other two sides.

In one way or another, the presenters should be able to explain that both BX and XC must be more than one-fourth of BC.

In other words, X must fall in the "center half" of $\overline{BC}$ in order that a triangle can be formed. (If BX is less than $\frac{1}{4}$ of BC, then $AB + BX < XC$, and if BX is more than $\frac{3}{4}$ of BC, then $AB + XC < BX$.)

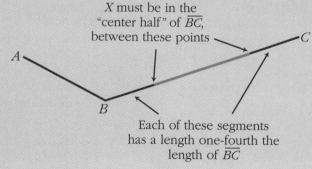

Thus, the probability is $\frac{1}{2}$ that a triangle can be made.

Note: If students raise the question of what happens if X is exactly at the $\frac{1}{4}$ or $\frac{3}{4}$ point along $\overline{BC}$, you can talk about the fact that when there are infinitely many equally likely results, the probability of any single result is equal to zero. Such a statement will probably raise as many questions as it answers, but it may lead to an interesting discussion.

Homework 19: To Measure a Tree
(see next page)

Tonight's homework is fairly open-ended. Its goal is to get students thinking about how to use ideas about similarity in concrete situations. You may want to take your class outside tomorrow to put the ideas in this assignment into real-life practice.

POW 19: Pool Pockets
(see page 146)

This POW is similar to *POW 16: Spiralaterals* in that it involves following paths and looking for patterns in the results. In tomorrow night's *Homework 20: A Few Special Bounces*, students will look at some special cases.

Discussion of this POW is scheduled for Day 25.

Homework 19   To Measure a Tree

This unit started with a problem about finding the length of a shadow. But other measurement ideas have come up as well.

You've seen how to measure the height of an object using a mirror. Now you will look at measuring the height of a tree.

One straightforward way to find the height of a tree is to climb to the tippy top and drop a long tape measure to the ground (while still holding one end) and have a friend on the ground read off how tall the tree is.

Although straightforward, that method has many potential difficulties (and dangers).

Fortunately, there's a less hazardous method—one that uses similar triangles.

Continued on next page

Interactive Mathematics Program

Your task in this assignment is to use your knowledge of similar triangles to invent a method for measuring a tree. Use the illustration above for ideas.

Write down what you'd have to know and how you'd use that information to figure out how high the tree is.

Identify clearly what similar triangles there are in the situation, and explain how they would fit into your method.

POW 19

Pool Pockets

Imagine a modified pool table in which the only pockets are those in the four corners.

The diagram at the right shows such a table as viewed from above.

This POW will use the view from above all the time, with different parts of the table labeled as in the next diagram.

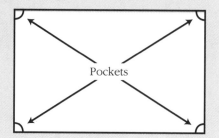

Pockets

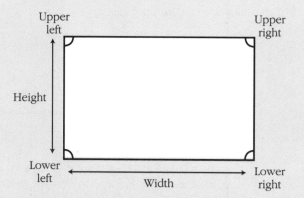

Upper left

Upper right

Height

Width

Lower left

Lower right

Next, imagine that a ball is hit from the lower left corner in a diagonal direction that forms a 45° angle with the sides, as shown in the diagram at the right.

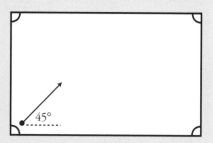

45°

Continued on next page

Interactive Mathematics Program

455

Finally, imagine that every time the ball hits an edge of the table, it bounces off, again at a 45° angle, and that it continues this way until it hits one of the corner pockets perfectly.

For example, using the previous diagram, the first few bounces of the ball would look like the diagram at the right.

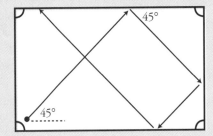

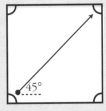

Of course, the path of the ball will depend on the shape of the table. For example, with a square table, the ball would go directly into the opposite corner without bouncing at all, as shown in the diagram at the left.

Your task in this POW is to investigate what happens to the ball and how this depends on the dimensions of the table.

You should make these assumptions.

- Both the height and the width of the table are whole number distances.

- The ball is always shot at an angle of 45°.

- The ball is always shot from the lower-left corner.

For example, you might look at these questions.

- Does the ball always hit a pocket eventually?

- If so, which pocket does it hit?

- If it does hit a pocket, how many times does it bounce before it hits the pocket?

You may have some other questions of your own.

You will probably find it very useful to have grid paper for your investigation, using the width of the squares on the grid paper as your unit of length. In that way, you'll be able to keep track more easily of the exact path of the ball.

Continued on next page

For example, the diagram to the right illustrates how you might use grid paper to show the path of the ball for a 3-by-5 table. The dotted lines represent the lines of the grid paper and the solid rectangle is the outline of the table. The diagonal lines with arrows show the path of the ball. At the end of the path, the ball is about to go into the pocket in the upper-right corner of the table.

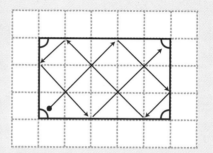

Happy bouncing!

Write-up

1. *Subject of Exploration:* Describe the subject that you are investigating. What questions do you want to explore?

2. *Information Gathering:* Basing your comments on your notes (which should be included with your write-up), state what happened in the specific cases you examined.

3. *Conclusions, Explanations, and Conjectures:* Describe any general observations you made or conclusions that you reached. Wherever possible, explain why the particular conclusions are true. That is, try to *prove* your general statements. But also include *conjectures*, that is, statements that you only *think* are true.

4. *Open Questions:* What questions do you have that you were not able to answer? What other investigations would you do if you had more time?

5. *Evaluation*

A Shadow of a Doubt

Students return to the unit problem and develop a general equation involving shadow length.

Mathematical Topics

- Continued work using similar triangles for indirect measurement
- Developing a general equation involving the variables from the unit problem
- Developing an algorithm for solving the general equation when specific values are given for *L, D,* and *H*

Outline of the Day

In Class

1. Discuss *Homework 19: To Measure a Tree*
2. Review the status of the unit problem
3. *A Shadow of a Doubt*
   - Students use similar triangles to find a general equation involving the variables from the unit problem

- Students develop an algorithm for solving this equation in specific cases
- The activity will be discussed on Day 21

At Home

Homework 20: A Few Special Bounces

1. Discussion of *Homework 19: To Measure a Tree*

You can ask students to take turns in their groups, each one explaining a method for measuring a tree, and then have them choose a method they might present to the class.

You might then ask a heart card student to present a method, and ask other students to present different methods or another version of the same method.

> *Note:* If logistics permit, you may want to take your class outdoors and try to apply the methods to a tree or other tall structure near the school.

There are several approaches to the problem, all based on similar triangles. The following material describes one method and suggests some questions you can ask as the discussion proceeds.

• *A sample method*

This approach begins by mentally drawing a line from the top of the tree, past the top of the person's head, to the ground, as shown below.

"What triangles are there in this diagram? Are they similar? Why?"

You can have students identify the triangles in the diagram and explain why the triangles are similar. It will probably be helpful to draw a schematic diagram such as this,

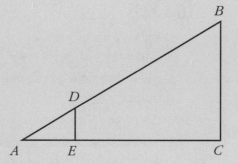

and perhaps to draw the large and small triangles separately, as shown below, in order to identify them more clearly.

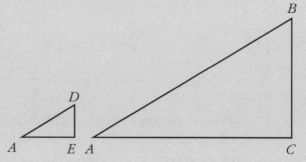

Students will probably use the "two-angle" method for demonstrating similarity. Specifically, the two triangles have angle *A* in common and both have a right angle.

You may want to have students identify the tree height and other lengths in terms of the diagram, and to have them clarify what they might be able to measure directly and more easily than the height of the tree.

They should see that the tree height is *BC* and that they might be able to measure each of these distances:

- the height of the person (*DE*)

- the distance along the ground from the person to the tree (*EC*)

- the distance along the ground from the end of the diagonal to the tree (*AC*)

If not many students got as far as identifying the similar triangles, you may want to let them work in their groups for a few minutes to develop a proportion that will help them find that height.

Students should come up with the proportion

$$\frac{DE}{BC} = \frac{AE}{AC}$$

or something equivalent.

Note: Finding the length of *AC* is not so easy, because one needs to first identify point *A*. One way a person could do this is to have a friend sight along the diagonal line that connects the top of the person's head and the top of the tree, and mark where this line hits the ground. A person could attempt to do this without help, but the result would probably be less accurate.

"Why are $\overline{DE}$ and $\overline{BC}$ corresponding sides? Why are $\overline{AE}$ and $\overline{AC}$ corresponding sides?"

You can use this as an opportunity to use the words opposite and adjacent as students describe corresponding sides in the triangles. For example, $\overline{DE}$ and $\overline{BC}$ are corresponding sides because they are both opposite angle A.

• *Using specific values*

Either as a follow-up to check understanding, or as a hint if students are having trouble seeing how to use the similar triangles, you can give the class specific values for the measurable distances. You should focus on *setting up* a proportion, rather than on finding the solution.

Here is a sample problem that students can work on.

The woman measuring the tree is 5 feet tall and is standing 20 feet from the tree. Her friend finds that the line of sight from the top of the tree past the top of the woman's head hits the ground just 4 feet beyond the woman.

How tall is the tree?

The term **line of sight** is a useful phrase in problems like these, and you might want to call attention to it. If there is enough time, you can have one or two groups present their solution to the whole class. Gauge the need for a discussion involving the whole class as you go from group to group helping and questioning.

• *Using shadows*

"How might you use shadows to work on this problem?"

You can bring students back to the unit problem by asking them how they might use shadows to work on this problem. As a further hint, suggest that they might be able to maneuver so that the length *AE* is actually a shadow.

The idea is that, if the sun is shining, you can stand so that you are just barely in the tree's shadow, so your shadow and the tree's shadow end at the same point. This way, the diagonal line will go to the end of the common shadow.

Shadows can be used for another overall approach to the problem as shown in the diagram below. You can stand anywhere and measure your height, the length of your shadow, and the length of the tree's shadow, and then use the following proportion:

$$\frac{\text{your height}}{\text{tree's height}} = \frac{\text{your shadow}}{\text{tree's shadow}}$$

2. Back to Shadows

Now that shadows have come up again, tell students that they are ready to achieve the goal set back at the beginning of the unit. You may want to do some review.

*"Can you describe
the diagram for
the lamppost
shadow problem?"*

You can begin by having students reconstruct the following diagram (developed on Day 3) or something equivalent:

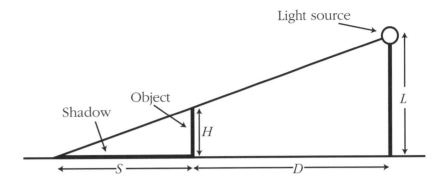

As needed, go over the meaning of each of the variables they were working with in their experiments on Days 4 through 6.

- *L* is the distance from the light source to the ground.

- *D* is the distance *along the ground* from the light source to the object casting the shadow.

- *H* is the height of the object casting the shadow.

- *S* is the length of the shadow.

Once the diagram and the variables have been reviewed, get the class to restate the goal itself. Here's the version that was included in the discussion on Day 3.

Unit Goal: To find a formula expressing *S*, the length of the shadow, in terms of the variables *L*, *D*, and *H*.

3. *A Shadow of a Doubt*
(see next page)

Students can now turn to the next activity, *A Shadow of a Doubt.* The emphasis in this activity is on the development and verification of an equation relating the four variables.

It is expected that students will see the similarity between the large and small triangles in the diagram above, and write a proportion like

$$\frac{S}{S+D} = \frac{H}{L}$$

or something equivalent (for example, $\frac{L}{H} = \frac{S+D}{S}$). *Note:* Some students may need a little help in identifying the horizontal side of the large triangle as $S + D$.

Groups need to come up with this proportion in order to do Questions 3 and 4 of the activity, so you will probably want to bring the class together to discuss Questions 1 and 2.

A Shadow of a Doubt

Can you now use the ideas of similarity to predict the length of a shadow without a shadow of a doubt?

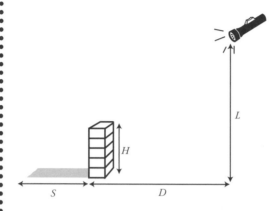

Recall these variables, shown in the diagram:

- L = the distance from the light source to the ground

- D = the distance along the ground from the light source to the object casting the shadow

- H = the height of the object casting the shadow

- S = the length of the shadow

Of course, in order to use similarity, you're going to have to find some triangles. They're hiding somewhere in the diagram above.

1. What triangles do you see in the diagram? Which of them are similar? Why must these triangles be similar?

2. Use your knowledge of similar triangles to write an equation that expresses a relationship between these four variables.

3. Students at Mystery High School did some experiments set up like the one above. As usual, there's a mystery about their work, because they forgot to write down the lengths of the shadows. Find the length of the shadow in each situation below.

   a. $L = 11, H = 5$, and $D = 12$

   b. $L = 15, H = 5$, and $D = 12$

   c. $L = 15, H = 5$, and $D = 60$

4. Write a description in words of how to find the length of a shadow when L, H, and D are given.

- *Expectations for Questions 3 and 4*

Students are not expected to get S in terms of the other variables by solving the general equation $\frac{S}{S+D} = \frac{H}{L}$. In tomorrow's activity, *More Triangles for Shadows,* they will see a

way to get S in terms of the other variables by using a less obvious pair of similar triangles.

In today's activity, however, you should expect them to solve for S in examples where they have numerical values for the other variables.

For example, in Question 3a, they have to solve something equivalent to this equation:

$$\frac{S}{S+12} = \frac{5}{11}$$

Because students have not explicitly studied the mechanics of manipulating an equation like this, they will have to solve the proportional equation in some other way. Trial and error (perhaps with the aid of their calculators) will probably be the most common approach. (The particular values given in Question 3 all lead to whole-number solutions for S. You may want to make up another problem that does not have a whole-number solution.)

Question 4 gives students an opportunity to verbalize the techniques that they use in Question 3.

You may want to give transparencies to some students with interesting or very clear approaches. Discussion of this activity is scheduled for tomorrow.

Jackie Hernandez, Aaron Gago, Maria Valenzuela, and Dolly Quintana compare notes after measuring the distance from a mirror to a light pole.

Homework 20 A Few Special Bounces

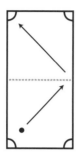

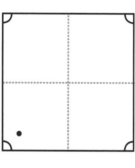

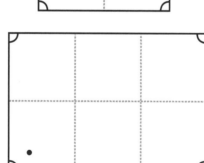

POW 19: Pool Pockets asks you to consider all possible tables with whole-number dimensions.

That's a lot of cases, so this assignment will get you started with a simpler version.

Specifically, you will consider all tables that have a height of exactly two units. (Remember that the width is supposed to be a whole number.)

The first three such tables are shown at the left, and the path of the ball has been drawn for the first of these tables.

Be sure to consider not just these three, but all tables with a height of two units.

What happens to the ball on these tables? Consider the specific questions posed in the POW and make up some others of your own.

Homework 20:
A Few Special Bounces

Tonight's homework assignment gives students some special cases of their POW to explore.

Days 21-26

The Lamp and the Sun

This page in the student book introduces Days 21 through 26.

You're about to solve the lamp shadow problem, and get a rather nice formula expressing the length of the shadow in terms of other variables.

But here comes another problem—the sun shadow! As you solve this problem, you will be finishing the unit and Year 1 as well.

Your portfolio for this unit asks you to look back over the entire year.

Mike Dominguez experiments with trigonometric functions on his calculator.

More Triangles for Shadows

Students use an auxiliary line to get an equation for shadow length in terms of other variables.

Mathematical Topics

- Finishing development of a general equation involving the variables from the unit problem
- Using an auxiliary line to get a simpler equation for the shadow problem

Outline of the Day

In Class

1. Discuss *Homework 20: A Few Special Bounces*
   - Confirm that students understand the POW
2. Discuss *A Shadow of a Doubt*
   - Elicit the equation $\frac{S}{S+D} = \frac{H}{L}$
3. *More Triangles for Shadows*
   - Students use an auxiliary line to get a simpler equation for the shadow problem

4. Discuss *More Triangles for Shadows*
   - Develop the equation $S = \frac{DH}{L-H}$
5. Point out that students still have to solve the sun shadow problem

At Home

Homework 21: The Sun Shadow Problem

Discuss With Your Colleagues

Isn't the Unit Over Yet?

Today your students will find a formula for the shadow length in terms of the other variables, yet the unit continues for several more days, introducing new concepts such as trigonometric functions.

Does this pose problems for you as a teacher (especially if this is happening at the end of the school year)?

1. Discussion of *Homework 20: A Few Special Bounces*

The purpose of this assignment is to get students started on the POW and to make sure they understand the situation. You may want to let them share some of their results on the special case described in the homework, or you may prefer to let them save their results for the POW discussion on Day 25.

Perhaps as a minimum, you should confirm that students found that the ball hit a pocket in every case.

You should remind students, if necessary, that they are to consider other questions, not simply which pocket the ball lands in. For example, they should explore the number of bounces needed for different tables.

2. Discussion of *A Shadow of a Doubt*

The discussion of this activity will lead to the achievement of the unit goal, so be sure that students have plenty of opportunity to raise questions about the general process.

"How can you use the shadow diagram to get an equation relating S, L, D, and H?"

"What similar triangles are involved?"

You can begin by having a spade card student summarize how to use the shadow diagram to get a general equation relating the four variables. Be sure to include discussion of what the similar triangles are and how students can be sure that the triangles are similar.

Then you can have other spade card students present the different examples from Question 3. If appropriate to their presentations, use this as an occasion to have students review ideas from *Homework 13: Inventing Rules*.

The discussion of Question 4, and the decision where to proceed next, will depend on what students did with this question.

- If they were able to solve the equation $\frac{S}{S+D} = \frac{H}{L}$ to get S in terms of L, D, and H, you should celebrate their achievement with considerable fanfare. They have accomplished the unit goal as

developed and refined back on Day 3. In this case, you may choose to omit the next activity, *More Triangles for Shadows,* and let students start work on *Homework 21: The Sun Shadow Problem.* (You may want to let students work on *More Triangles for Shadows* anyway to get some further insight into the problem.)

• If students could solve the shadow problem only when they had specific numbers for *L*, *D*, and *H*, and did not yet have the algebra skills to get a general solution, you can have them move into the next activity, *More Triangles for* *Shadows*, which will provide a geometric tool for accomplishing the unit goal. Don't push for an algorithm for solving the proportions, since that was not the intended focus of *A Shadow* *of a Doubt*.

3. *More Triangles* *for Shadows*
(see next page)

If students did not get a general solution for *S* in terms of *L*, *D*, and *H*, introduce this activity by pointing out what they have achieved and what is still missing.

Presumably, they have an equation relating the four variables, which probably looks like $\frac{S}{S+D} = \frac{H}{L}$, and can find *S* when they are given specific values of the variables *L*, *D*, and *H*.

They may not yet have a general formula for *S* as a function of those variables. That is, they have not achieved the goal of getting a formula of the general type $S = f(L, D, H)$.

You can point out that even with specific values for *L*, *D*, and *H*, solving an equation like $\frac{S}{S+D} = \frac{H}{L}$ for *S* is complicated by the fact that *S* appears in two parts of the equation.

You can tell students that they will learn some algebra techniques in Year 2 of the IMP curriculum that will allow them to get a formula for *S* from the general equation, but that, for now, they can use the geometry to help avoid this dilemma.

With that introduction (most of which is summarized in the activity itself), let students work in groups on *More Triangles for Shadows*.

"Is there another triangle you can find in this diagram that would help?"

Hold off giving hints for as long as possible. If necessary, suggest drawing another line in the diagram. If something more specific is needed, you can ask them to look for a triangle that has a side of length *D* rather than *S* + *D*.

This activity basically involves an "aha!" of insight in order to draw the right additional line. You need not wait for every group to experience the insight, but try to give the class a sense of collective accomplishment about this. For example, once a couple of groups have seen how to find the correct other triangle, you may want to give the remaining groups the diagram so that they can all do the final algebra.

More Triangles for Shadows

By now, you have probably developed a diagram similar to the one shown here in order to represent the shadow problem.

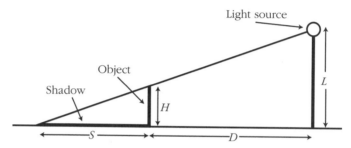

In terms of this diagram, the length of a shadow (*S*) depends on the height of the light source (*L*), on the height of the object casting the shadow (*H*), and on the distance along the ground from that object to the light source (*D*).

Your goal is to develop an algebraic expression for *S* in terms of *L, H*, and *D*. In other words, you would like to find a function *f* so that $S = f(L, D, H)$.

You may have used similar triangles to develop an equation involving these four variables. For example, if you compare the small triangle in the diagram to the large triangle, you might get the equation

$$\frac{S}{S+D} = \frac{H}{L}$$

The fact that *S* appears in two places in this equation complicates the process of using this equation to get a general expression for *S* in terms of the other variables.

So in this assignment, your task is to find another way to use similar triangles so that using proportions gives you a simpler initial equation.

In particular, see if you can find a pair of similar triangles in the diagram so that the variable *S* appears in only one place in the equation for proportionality. Once you get that simpler equation, use it to find the long-sought expression for *S* in terms of *L, H*, and *D*.

4. Discussion of *More Triangles for Shadows*

You might let a volunteer describe how to get the equation. Essentially, the key is to draw a new horizontal line, as shown in the diagram below, and to use the similarity of the two small triangles.

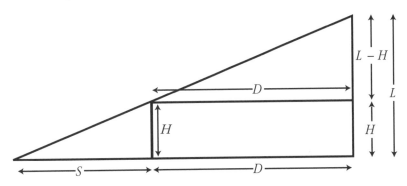

"How do you know that these triangles are similar?"

Get students to articulate how they know that these triangles are similar. This will probably involve their work with corresponding angles from the Day 15 activity, *More About Angles*.

Once they have the diagram above and realize which triangles to use, all the groups should be able to get an equation like this one from the proportionality property:

$$\frac{S}{D} = \frac{H}{L-H}$$

The final step is to get them to solve this equation for S. They should be able to get something like

$$S = \frac{DH}{L-H}$$

or, equivalently,

$$S = D\frac{H}{L-H}$$

At this point, give a cheer—the unit goal has been achieved!

5. What About Sun Shadows?

Students may notice that, although they have achieved the unit goal, there is still more material in the unit. Remind them that what they have solved is the *lamp shadow* problem, and that there is still a *sun shadow* problem to work on.

Tonight's homework asks them to begin thinking about how they might solve such a problem.

Homework 21

The Sun Shadow Problem

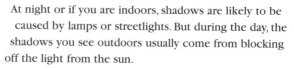

At night or if you are indoors, shadows are likely to be caused by lamps or streetlights. But during the day, the shadows you see outdoors usually come from blocking off the light from the sun.

For such a "sun shadow," it doesn't make much sense to talk about the height of the light source off the ground or the distance along the ground from the light source to the object casting the shadow.

In other words, the variables L and D are pretty meaningless for sun shadows.

So what does the length of a sun shadow depend on? What are the relevant variables? At what time of day would a shadow be the longest and when would it be the shortest?

Speculate on these questions (and any others you want to add). Think about how one might go about expressing the length of a shadow in terms of those variables.

Write down any conjectures or ideas you have on these issues.

*Homework 21:
The Sun Shadow
Problem*

This assignment should get students thinking about the last stage of the unit.

The Return of the Tree

Students use angles, similarity, and a scale diagram to measure the height of a tree.

Mathematical Topics

- Stating the sun shadow problem clearly
- Using a scale drawing for indirect measurement

Outline of the Day

In Class

1. Discuss *Homework 21: The Sun Shadow Problem*
   - Bring out the importance of the **angle of elevation** of the sun

2. *The Return of the Tree*
   - Students use a scale drawing to do indirect measurement

3. Discuss *The Return of the Tree*

At Home

Homework 22: Right Triangle Ratios

1. Discussion of Homework 21: The Sun Shadow Problem

Let students share their ideas as a whole class. The goal here is to identify the key variables, but not yet to get a solution to the problem. (The solution of the sun shadow problem is achieved in the activity *The Sun Shadow* on Day 24, after the introduction of trigonometric functions.)

Students should recognize that the height of the object casting the shadow, which has been labeled *H* before, is still an important variable.

If students mention "time of day" or "position on the globe" as factors, ask: "Why do these factors affect the length of a shadow?"

They may also mention *time of day* and *position on the globe* as possible variables that could affect the length of a shadow. If so, ask why these matter, trying to get students to recognize that they affect the *angle* at which the sun hits an object. That is, coax them along until they see that the angle of the sun's position in the sky can be used as the crucial other variable.

It may help to bring out that at noon, the shadows are the shortest, and that toward dusk or shortly after dawn, the shadows are the longest.

If students have trouble picturing the desired angle, you might suggest that they imagine looking straight ahead and then tilt their heads as if looking up toward the sun. The amount of "tilt" needed represents the angle on which they should focus.

You may want to culminate this discussion by introducing a generic diagram similar to the one below. Introduce the term **angle of elevation** for the "tilt" represented by θ in this diagram.

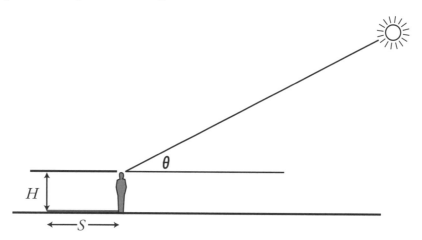

In terms of this diagram, students should recognize that they are looking for a way to express S as a function of H and θ. That is, they want a formula for a function g so that $S = g(H, \theta)$.

> *Reminder:* If you didn't introduce students to the Greek letter θ on Day 3, you can do so now.

or

The Return of the Tree

Woody is really interested in trees, and he was pretty excited when he learned the ideas from *Homework 19: To Measure a Tree.*

Now Woody has found a new way to measure a tree. (You probably can't wait to hear about it!)

First he measured the height from the ground to his eye. That was 5 feet.

Then he used a protractor to measure the angle between the horizontal and his line of sight up to the top of the tree. That turned out to be 70°.

Finally, he measured his distance from the tree. That was 12 feet.

That's all the information that Woody needed. Using these measurements, he figured out how tall the tree was. So you, with the help of your trusty protractor and your understanding of similarity, should be able to figure it out also.

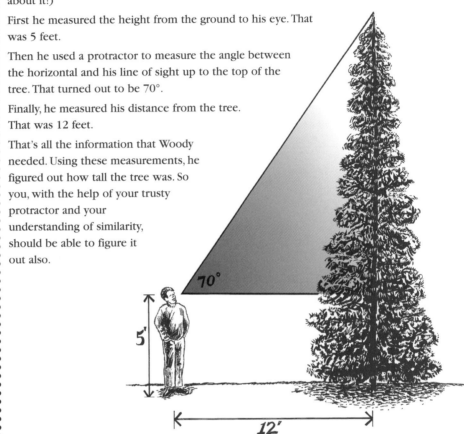

2. *The Return of the Tree*

Tell students that before looking at the general sun shadow problem, they will return to the tree-measuring problem in today's activity, *The Return of the Tree.* Ask students to work on this problem in their groups.

Students will probably end up making an accurate scale drawing to figure out the height of the tree. That is, they will probably draw a right triangle with a base angle of 70°, and make the base 12 centimeters, 12 inches, or 12 boxes on grid paper.

They can then measure the height of the tree on the scale drawing. (It should be about 33 centimeters, inches, or boxes. They will have to adjust this value to take Woody's height into account.)

Students may need some hints on this activity, but they do have all the tools and concepts needed.

3. Discussion of *The Return of the Tree*

When all the students have made the triangle and figured out the height for 70°, ask them to compare their answers. Settle on an approximate answer. Be sure that they add the 5 feet between Woody's eye and the ground.

Ask the class how they knew that the distance they found using their scale drawings would be the actual distance. Try to get to these particulars.

"How did you know you were drawing a similar triangle?"

- How did students know they were drawing a similar triangle? (Possible answer: If two angles of one triangle are equal to two angles of another triangle, then the triangles are similar; here both triangles have a 90° angle and a 70° angle.)

"What about similar triangles allows you to use information from one triangle to gain information about another?"

- What is it about similar triangles that allows students to use information from one triangle to gain information about another? (Possible answer: If two triangles are similar, then the ratios of the sides within one triangle are equal to the ratios of the sides within the other.)

"Where do you see scale drawings used?"

You can discuss with the class the concept of a scale drawing. Ask them where they see scale drawings used. Maps, assembly instructions, architectural designs, and public transportation routes might be mentioned.

"What do scale drawings have in common?"

You can also ask them what scale drawings have in common. Some basic points to get across are that a scale drawing is a different-sized version of an original and that distances measured on a scale drawing can be easily converted to the distances on the original.

You may want to ask them to bring some scale drawings to class tomorrow to discuss how accurately they are drawn. You may need to point out that some maps are distorted to allow for better readability.

• *(Optional) Use real trees*

If time and logistics permit, have your class apply the ideas of this activity to trees or other structures near your school.

Homework 22: Right Triangle Ratios

(see next page)

Tonight's homework assignment provides the basis for tomorrow's introduction of the three primary trigonometric functions for right triangles.

You should emphasize to students that they need to measure their lengths (in Question 1) as carefully as possible, in order to get fairly accurate results for the ratios in Question 2. (If their work is sloppy, it won't lead to conclusions that support the introduction of the trigonometric functions.)

Jennifer Brenneman will add the unit's cover letter to her personalized portfolio.

Homework 22 Right Triangle Ratios

Many of the problems you've worked on, including the basic diagram for the shadow problems, have involved right angles.

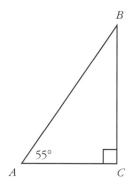

You've also seen that ideas of similarity involve ratios of sides of triangles.

So it's natural to think about ratios of sides within right triangles.

1. Carefully draw a right triangle *ABC* with a right angle at *C* and with a 55° angle at *A,* such as the one at the right. (You should make your triangle larger than the one at the right so your measurement error will be less significant.)

   Record the lengths of the three sides of your triangle.

In *Homework 12: Very Special Triangles,* you were introduced to this terminology:

   • Side $\overline{AB}$ is called the **hypotenuse** of this right triangle.

   • Side $\overline{BC}$ is called the leg **opposite** angle *A.*

   • Side $\overline{AC}$ is called the leg **adjacent to** angle *A.*

2. Find each of the ratios below. If your measurements in Question 1 involved fractions of a unit, convert your fractions to decimals and use those decimal values to compute the ratios.

   a. $\dfrac{\text{length of leg opposite angle } A}{\text{length of hypotenuse}}$

   b. $\dfrac{\text{length of leg adjacent to angle } A}{\text{length of hypotenuse}}$

   c. $\dfrac{\text{length of leg opposite angle } A}{\text{length of leg adjacent to angle } A}$

3. Do you think that your classmates will get the same results for Questions 1 and 2 that you got? Explain in detail why or why not.

The Trigonometric Functions

Students are introduced to the trigonometric functions and then use them in familiar situations.

Mathematical Topics

- Introduction of the trigonometric functions
- Using trigonometric functions in familiar problem situations

Outline of the Day

In Class

1. Discuss *Homework 22: Right Triangle Ratios*
   - Bring out that if two right triangles have an acute angle in common, then the triangles are similar
   - Post this principle
2. Have students read *Sin, Cos, and Tan Buttons Revealed*
   - Focus on the three primary trigonometric functions
   - Post the definitions

- Bring out the similarity between trigonometric notation and function notation
3. *The Tree and the Pendulum*
   - Students apply trigonometric functions to simple, familiar situations
4. Discuss *The Tree and the Pendulum*

At Home

Homework 23: Smokey and the Dude

Discuss With Your Colleagues

Trigonometry in Ninth Grade?

The introduction of the trigonometric functions in ninth grade is one of the products of IMP's integrated curriculum.

What should you expect from students at this point? What else will they learn about trigonometry?

You and colleagues may want to look at some later IMP units to see how students will build on this introduction. Ideas about right triangle trigonometry will be used in important ways in *Do Bees Build It Best?* (Year 2) and *Orchard Hideout* (Year 3). Students will extend these ideas to the concepts of circular functions in *High Dive* (Year 4), develop some standard formulas, such as the angle sum formula $\sin(A + B) = \sin A \cos B + \cos A \sin B$, in *As the Cube Turns* (Year 4), and learn about the law of sines and the law of cosines in *Know How* (Year 4).

1. Discussion of Homework 22: Right Triangle Ratios

Have students share their numerical results with group members, and bring the class together for a discussion of what they discovered.

They should have found that even though group members may have drawn triangles of very different sizes, the ratios will come out essentially equal. In other words, they may get different values in Question 1, but should get approximately the same answers for Questions 2a through 2c.

> *Note:* If this is not the case, you may need to discuss the degree of accuracy of their measurements or make sure they have found the right ratios.

"Why did you get approximately the same ratios?"

Ask for an explanation of the fact that their ratios are equal. Students should come up with the principle of similarity and should be able to explain why the triangles drawn are all similar to each other. That is, they should see that the triangles are all right triangles, so each one has a right angle. In addition, the triangles are all drawn with a 55° angle. Because all the triangles have two angles in common, the triangles must all be similar.

If needed, review how the ratios here are connected to the idea introduced in *Homework 16: Ins and Outs of Proportion*. That is, although similarity is defined in terms of ratios of corresponding sides of different triangles, having these ratios equal is equivalent to having corresponding ratios of sides within the triangles be equal. This idea applies to any family of similar triangles—not just to right triangles. But with right triangles, a "similarity family" can be specified by giving a single acute angle.

*"Is there anything
special about 55°,
or does this
illustrate a more
general principle?"*

For emphasis, ask the class if there is anything special about 55° for this problem, and ask if they can state a general principle. The goal is to get them to say similar to this statement:

If two right triangles have an acute angle in common, then the triangles are similar.

Post this principle alongside the related result from Day 13 (which says that if two angles of one triangle are equal to two angles of another, then the triangles are similar). Bring out that this new principle is just a special case of the earlier one.

If it isn't yet clear, bring out that this means that ratios such as those defined in the homework depend only on angle *A*, and not on the particular right triangle drawn with that angle.

2. For Reference: Sin, Cos, and Tan Buttons Revealed

(see next page)

With some fanfare, tell students that these ratios within right triangles are the fundamental idea of **trigonometry**. You may want to point out that these ratios are important because right triangles are so important.

You can direct students to the material in *Sin, Cos, and Tan Buttons Revealed* and go over the definitions. *Note:* This is reference material, not an activity.

You should post these definitions in a prominent place.

You can tell students that people just figured out what these ratios were for a wide variety of angles, wrote their results down in a table, and then published the table of trigonometric values. Tell them that the information in those tables is now more easily available from calculators.

Have students find sin 55°, cos 55°, and tan 55° on their calculators and compare the values to their results on Questions 2a, 2b, and 2c, respectively, of the homework. If there are significant discrepancies, you should have them figure out the reasons.

You should remind students that the terms *opposite* and *adjacent* are always used in relation to a specific angle. They should realize, for example, that side $\overline{BC}$ is adjacent to angle *B* as well as opposite angle *A*. (*Homework 24: Your Opposite Is My Adjacent* uses this fact to develop some formulas about trigonometric functions.)

Sin, Cos, and Tan Buttons Revealed

Did you ever wonder what those keys on your calculator that say "sin," "cos," and "tan" are all about? Well, here's where you find out.

You've seen that, whenever two right triangles have another angle in common, the triangles must be similar, and so the corresponding ratios of lengths of sides within those triangles are equal.

These ratios depend only on that common acute angle, and each ratio of lengths within the right triangle has a name. The study and use of these ratios is part of a branch of mathematics called **trigonometry.**

Suppose you are given an acute angle (in other words, an angle between 0° and 90°).

You can create a right triangle in which one of the acute angles is equal to that given angle. Suppose you label that triangle as shown in the diagram below, so that ∠A is equal to the acute angle you started with.

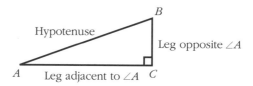

The trigonometric ratios are then defined as explained on the following pages. The principles of similarity guarantee that these ratios will be the same for *every* right triangle that has an acute angle the same size as ∠A.

Continued on next page

• *Trigonometric notation is like function notation*

As a side note, bring out that trigonometric functions are written in a way that is similar to the function notation introduced in *The Pit and the Pendulum*. That is, notation such as "sin 55°" starts with the name for the function (although here, it is a full name or an abbreviation of that name instead of a letter like *f* or *g*) and then gives the input to the function. (One usually doesn't use parentheses around the input for trigonometric functions.)

Sine of an Angle

The **sine** of ∠A is the ratio of the length of the leg opposite ∠A to the length of the hypotenuse. The sine of ∠A is abbreviated as **sin A**. For example, in △RST below, the leg opposite ∠R has length 4, and the hypotenuse has length 7, so sin R = $\frac{4}{7}$.

In summary

$$\sin A = \frac{\text{length of leg opposite } \angle A}{\text{length of hypotenuse}}$$

or simply,

$$\sin A = \frac{\text{opposite}}{\text{hypotenuse}}$$

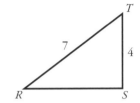

Cosine of an Angle

The **cosine** of ∠A is the ratio of the length of the leg adjacent to ∠A to the length of the hypotenuse. The cosine of ∠A is abbreviated as **cos A**. For example, in △UVW below, the leg adjacent to ∠U has length 3, and the hypotenuse has length 5, so cos U = $\frac{3}{5}$.

In summary

$$\cos A = \frac{\text{length of leg adjacent to } \angle A}{\text{length of hypotenuse}}$$

or simply,

$$\cos A = \frac{\text{adjacent}}{\text{hypotenuse}}$$

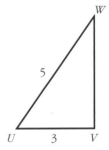

Tangent of an Angle

The **tangent** of ∠A is the ratio of the length of the leg opposite ∠A to the length of the leg adjacent to ∠A. The tangent of ∠A is abbreviated as **tan A**. For example, in △HKL on the following page, the leg opposite ∠H has length 2, and the leg adjacent to ∠H has length 6, so tan H = $\frac{2}{6}$.

Continued on next page

You may want, for a while, to write sin (55°), with the parentheses, as a way of emphasizing this similarity. At the same time, you may want to make a point of the fact that sin 55° (with or without parentheses) is not a product of sin and 55, but that the number 55 is acting as the input to a function in this context.

In summary

$$\tan A = \frac{\text{length of leg opposite } \angle A}{\text{length of leg adjacent to } \angle A}$$

or simply,

$$\tan A = \frac{\text{opposite}}{\text{adjacent}}$$

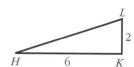

Trigonometric Functions on a Calculator

Any scientific calculator or graphing calculator has keys that will give you the values of these functions for any angle.

In some calculators, you enter the size of the angle and then push the appropriate trigonometric key, while for other calculators, you do the opposite.

Caution: You have been measuring angles using *degrees* as the unit of measurement, but there are other units for measuring angles. Most calculators that work with trigonometric functions have a *mode* key that you can set to "deg."

The Other Ratios

There are three other ratios of side lengths within a right triangle, in addition to the sine, the cosine, and the tangent. These other ratios are used less often and usually do not have their own calculator keys.

Each is the reciprocal of one of the three ratios already defined. Here are the definitions of those other ratios.

$$\text{cotangent } A = \frac{1}{\text{tangent } A}$$

$$\text{secant } A = \frac{1}{\text{cosine } A}$$

$$\text{cosecant } A = \frac{1}{\text{sine } A}$$

They are abbreviated, respectively, as **cot A, sec A,** and **csc A.**

3. *The Tree and the Pendulum*
(see next page)

These two problems are intended to illustrate the use of trigonometric functions to solve familiar problems. Students' work on this activity should give you a sense of how well students have absorbed the basics of trigonometry.

It is likely that students' main difficulty with these problems will be deciding which trigonometric function to use. You can help them refer to the definitions and clarify the meanings of the terms *opposite* and *adjacent*.

4. Discussion of *The Tree and the Pendulum*

You may choose to let volunteers present their work.

On Question 1, students should be able to set up a diagram like the one below, and to see that the ratio $\frac{x}{12}$ must be equal to tan 70°, so that $x = 12 \tan 70° \approx 32.97$. Adding in the distance from Woody's eye to the ground (5 feet) gives the height of the tree as approximately 38 feet.

Question 2 involves the use of the sine function, and students should be able to set up an equation like sin 30°=$\frac{d}{30}$, which is equivalent to $d = 30 \sin 30°$, so the distance is 15 feet. (*Note:* A supplemental problem, *Exactly One-Half!*, asks students to prove that sin 30° is exactly 0.5.)

70°

12 feet

x

The Tree and the Pendulum

1. Now that you have been introduced to the definitions of the trigonometric functions, it's time to look again at the situation described in *The Return of the Tree*.

   Here are the key facts again.

   • Woody was 12 feet from the tree.

   • Woody's line of sight to the top of the tree was at an angle of 70° up from horizontal.

   • Woody's eye was 5 feet off the ground.

   Describe how Woody could find the height of the tree using trigonometry and these measurements.

Continued on next page

2. You can also apply trigonometry to the pendulum from *The Pit and the Pendulum*.

For example, suppose a 30-foot pendulum has an initial amplitude of 30°, as shown at the right.

How far is the bob from the center line when the pendulum starts? In other words, what is the distance labeled *d*?

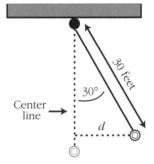

(By the way, although the last syllable of the word *trigonometry* sounds like "tree," the origin of the word really has nothing to do with trees. The word comes from Greek and combines the word *trigonon*, which means "triangle," and the suffix *-metria*, which means "measurement.")

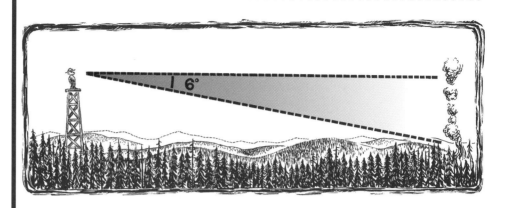

Homework 23   Smokey and the Dude

Reminder: Be sure to check that your calculator is set to use *degrees*. (There is probably a *mode* key to fix this setting.)

1. Smokey the Bear

Smokey the Bear is atop a 100-foot tower, looking out over a fairly level area for careless people who might start fires.

Suddenly, he sees a fire starting. He marks down the direction of the fire, but he also needs to know how far away from the tower the fire is.

To figure out this distance, Smokey grabs his handy protractor. Since he is high up on top of the tower, he has to look slightly downward toward the fire. He finds that his line of sight to the fire is at an angle of 6° below horizontal, as shown in the diagram above. (*Note:* This diagram is not to scale.)

     a. How far is Smokey from the fire?

     b. How far is the base of Smokey's tower from the fire?

Continued on next page

Homework 23: Smokey and the Dude

Students will need a scientific calculator with trigonometric functions to do this assignment. Be sure they realize that their calculators at home may work differently from those they use in class. You should remind them to check the mode setting of their calculators.

2. *Dude on a Cliff*

Shredding Charlene is out surfing and catches the eye of her friend, Dave the Dude, who is standing at the top of a vertical cliff. The angle formed by Charlene's line of sight and the horizontal measures 28°. Charlene is 50 meters out from the bottom of the cliff. Charlene and Dave are both 1.7 meters tall. They are both 16 years old. The surfboard is level with the base of the cliff. How high is the cliff?

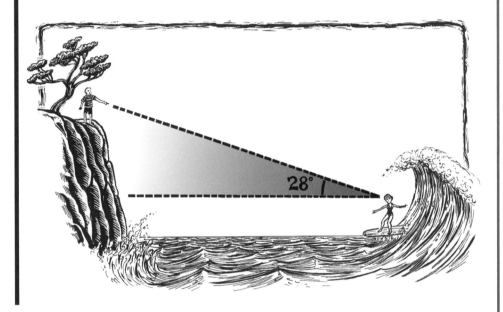

For your information: A surfer who has done outlandish maneuvers on a wave is said to have *shredded* it, hence the reference in Question 2 to "Shredding Charlene."

Students solve the sun shadow problem using trigonometry.

Mathematical Topics

- Problem solving using trigonometric ratios
- Solving the sun shadow problem

Outline of the Day

In Class

1. Select presenters for tomorrow's discussion of *POW 19: Pool Pockets*

2. Discuss *Homework 23: Smokey and the Dude*

3. *The Sun Shadow*
   - Students find a formula for the length of a sun shadow in terms of the sun's angle of elevation

4. Discuss *The Sun Shadow*
   - Develop the formula $S = \dfrac{H}{\tan \theta}$

At Home

Homework 24: *Your Opposite Is My Adjacent*

1. POW Presentation Preparation

Presentations of *POW 19: Pool Pockets* are scheduled for tomorrow. Choose three students to make POW presentations, and give them overhead transparencies and pens to take home to use in their preparations.

2. Discussion of Homework 23: Smokey and the Dude

"What triangle are you using?"

Discuss Question 1 of the homework as a class. Have students clarify what triangle they are using, since there are really two identical triangles in the problem, labeled Triangle I and Triangle II in the diagram below.

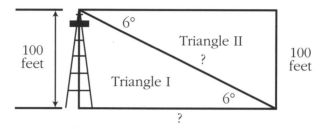

If students work with Triangle I, they will need to realize that the angle at the lower right is 6°. If they work with Triangle II, they will need to realize that the vertical side at the right is 100 feet long and that the length of the horizontal side at the top is the same as the distance from the base of the tower to the fire.

Based on one or the other of these triangles, students should have been able to come up with the relationships

$$\sin 6° = \frac{100 \text{ feet}}{\text{distance from Smokey to fire}}$$

and

$$\tan 6° = \frac{100 \text{ feet}}{\text{distance from base of tower to fire}}$$

If students raise questions about the effect of Smokey's own height, use your judgment about how to incorporate the issue into the discussion.

Students should have been able to find the values of sin 6° and tan 6° from their calculators, and then, with some trial and error, they should have been able find the desired distances. It's about 951.4 feet from the fire to the base of the tower, and about 956.7 feet from the fire to Smokey. (Students may be amazed at how close the two values are.)

Some students may have used the complementary angle, 84°, in this problem. (The term *complementary* will be introduced in tomorrow's discussion of tonight's homework.) For example, they could find the distance from the fire to the base of the tower by using the equation

$$\tan 84° = \frac{\text{distance to fire}}{100 \text{ feet}}$$

so the distance from the fire to the base of the tower is 100 · tan 84°, which is again about 951.4 feet.

• *Question 2*

Depending on the success of the discussion of Question 1, you may decide to skip Question 2, to allow students to rework Question 2 in light of the class discussion, or to have students go straight to the next activity, *The Sun Shadow*.

For your convenience: The basic equation for Question 2 is

$$\tan 28° = \frac{\text{height of cliff}}{50 \text{ meters}}$$

which results in

height of cliff ≈ 26.6 meters

(Since Dave's and Charlene's heights are equal, they cancel out in analyzing the problem.)

3. *The Sun Shadow*
(see next page)

Let students now put their knowledge of trigonometry to use solving the general sun shadow problem.

If students need a hint to get started, you may want to review the general diagram (see Day 22) or suggest that they start with specific values for H and θ. The latter hint may be especially useful in helping them solve the trigonometric equation for S in terms of H and θ.

Students may also need a hint that the angle of elevation from their eyes to the sun is the same as the angle in the triangle formed by their bodies and their shadows (both labeled θ in the diagram that accompanies the discussion of this activity).

4. Discussion of *The Sun Shadow*

There are essentially three steps to solving this problem, and you may want to have several presentations on each step of the analysis:

- Setting up a clear diagram, appropriately labeled
- Using the diagram to get an equation involving S, H, and θ
- Solving this equation for S in terms of H and θ

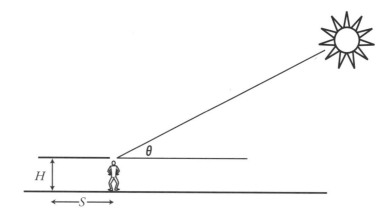

The Sun Shadow

Suppose you are standing outdoors on a bright, sunny day.

You look up toward the sun and estimate the angle of the sun's elevation.

In other words, you measure the angle shown as θ in the diagram above.

How can you find the length of your shadow (S) using this angle and your own height (H)?

Once students have a diagram like the one below, they will probably start with the equation $\tan \theta = \frac{H}{S}$, and then need to solve for S. As suggested earlier, it may be helpful to work this out once or twice with specific values for H and θ, and then use those examples to develop the general expression $S = \frac{H}{\tan \theta}$.

This work essentially completes the unit problem, and the result should be given appropriate fanfare.

Note: It's possible that some students will use the cotangent function and get $S = H \cot \theta$. This is certainly correct as well, and you can use this expression to review the definition of cotangent as the reciprocal of tangent.

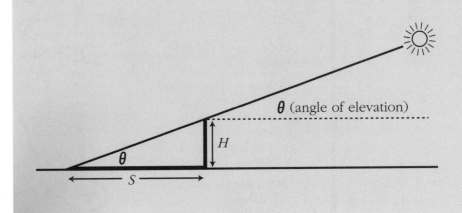

θ (angle of elevation)

H

θ

S

Homework 24   Your Opposite Is My Adjacent

Every right triangle has two acute angles. You can learn some interesting facts about trigonometry by using both of them.

Use the labeling in $\triangle ABC$ below to answer the questions.

1. What relationship must exist between angles A and B? (*Hint:* If you know one of these two angles, how can you find the other?)

2. Express the ratio $\frac{BC}{AB}$ in two ways:

   a. as the sine, cosine, or tangent of $\angle A$

   b. as the sine, cosine, or tangent of $\angle B$

3. a. Use your results from Questions 1 and 2 to write a general formula for the sine of an angle as the cosine of a related angle.

   b. Write a similar general formula for the cosine of an angle as the sine of a related angle.

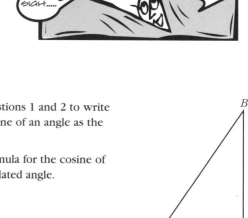

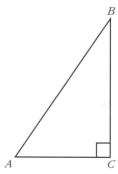

Homework 24:
Your Opposite Is
My Adjacent

This assignment focuses on the relationship between the sine and cosine functions.

POW 19 Presentations

Mathematical Topics

- Complementary angles
- Developing the formula $\sin \theta = \cos (90° - \theta)$ and related formulas
- Looking for patterns in a geometric problem

Outline of the Day

In Class

1. Discuss *Homework 24: Your Opposite Is My Adjacent*
   - Clarify the terminology applied to right triangles
   - Develop the formula $\sin \theta = \cos (90° - \theta)$

2. Presentations of *POW 19: Pool Pockets*

At Home

Homework 25: Beginning Portfolio Selection

1. Discussion of Homework 24: Your Opposite Is My Adjacent

"How would you get one angle if you knew the other?"

You can let club card students make presentations on different parts of this assignment. (You may want to have volunteers on Question 4.)

In Question 1, students should see that $A + B = 90°$, although they might just as likely express this idea with equations like $A = 90° - B$ or $B = 90° - A$. For the discussion of Question 3, it will be helpful if students see this relationship in all three ways. You might bring out the equations $A = 90° - B$ and $B = 90° - A$ by asking how you would get one angle if you knew the other.

Introduce the term **complementary** for a pair of angles whose sum is 90°. As with earlier terminology, be sure students realize that this term cannot be used for a single angle, but describes a relationship between two angles. You may want to make a point of distinguishing *complementary* from *supplementary,* a term that was used on Day 15.

On Question 2, students should recognize that the ratio is both sin A and cos B. You can take this opportunity to point out that the "co" in *cosine* is the same beginning as in the word *complementary*.

This should probably lead in smoothly to Question 3, where students should put Questions 1 and 2 together to get the general formulas

$$\sin A = \cos (90° - A)$$

$$\cos B = \sin (90° - B)$$

Note: If students just wrote these relationships as sin A = cos B and cos B = sin A, you can have them go back to Question 1 and express B in terms of A for the first equation and express A in terms of B for the second.

"Can you find any similar relationships involving other trigonometric functions?"

As a follow-up to the discussion of Question 3 ask if students can find any similar relationships involving other trigonometric functions. One hint you can use is to have them express all six functions for both A and B as ratios of sides of the triangle, and then see which ratios come out the same. For example, both tan A and cot B are expressed as the ratio $\frac{BC}{AC}$.

You can point out that each of the "plain" functions—sine, tangent, and secant—for $\angle A$ gives the same ratio as the corresponding "co" function for $\angle B$. That is, in addition to the equation sin A = cos B found earlier, students should see that

$$\tan A = \cot B$$

$$\sec A = \csc B$$

You can introduce the formal term **cofunction** here as well. If you do, then also point out that the prefix "co" suggests the term *complementary* and that A and B are complementary angles. That is, a trigonometric function of an angle is equal to the corresponding cofunction of the complementary angle.

2. Presentations of POW 19: Pool Pockets

Have the three presenters describe their results for the POW.

There is no particular piece of knowledge that students need to gain from this POW, and so there are no particular results or conclusions that need to emerge from the discussion.

*"What other
conclusions did you
find? What other
questions did you
investigate?"*

When the presentations are over, ask if other students either have other conclusions to present or have other questions that they think are worthy of investigation.

One general idea that you can encourage is for students to organize their individual cases in different ways that might lead to insights.

For example, they might look at tables that all have a common height (as in *Homework 20: A Few Special Bounces*).

Another fruitful idea is to consider the relationship between height and width. For example, students might consider cases where the width is a multiple of the height.

They might also try organizing cases according to which pocket the ball eventually hits. For example, they might examine whether the cases in which the ball lands in the lower-right pocket have anything in common.

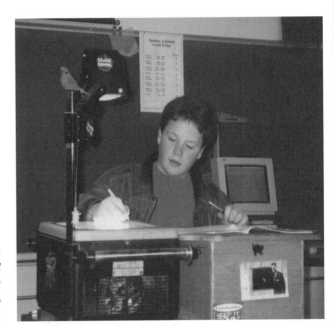

***Weston Pettigrew
uses the overhead
projector to present
his POW ideas to
the class.***

Homework 25   Beginning Portfolio Selection

As the first step in assembling your portfolio for *Shadows*, look back over the main unit problem.

One of the key ideas in this unit is the concept of *similarity*.

1. Explain what similarity means, both by giving an intuitive description and by using the formal definition.

2. Choose two or three activities in the unit that helped you understand this concept and use it. Explain why you chose those activities and how they contributed to your ideas about similarity.

474   Interactive Mathematics Program

Homework 25: Beginning Portfolio Selection

This assignment is the first stage in assembling student portfolios, a task that will continue tomorrow.

Portfolio Day

Mathematical Topics

• Reviewing the unit and preparing unit portfolios

Outline of the Day

In Class

1. Remind students that unit assessments will take place tomorrow and tomorrow night

2. *"Shadows" Portfolio*
   • Students write cover letters and assemble portfolios for the unit

At Home

Students complete portfolios and prepare for assessments

1. Reminder: Unit Assessments Tomorrow

Let students know that they will get their in-class and take-home unit assessments tomorrow. Their homework for tonight is to prepare for the assessments by reviewing the ideas of the unit. You may want to remind them to bring their notebooks to class tomorrow because the assessments are open book.

2. *"Shadows" Portfolio*

(see next page)

Tell students to read over the instructions in *"Shadows" Portfolio* carefully. Then they are to take out and review all of their work from the unit.

They will have completed part of the selection process in last night's homework, and their main task today is to write their cover letters. If students do not complete the task, you may want them to take the materials home and to finish compiling their portfolios for homework. Be sure that they bring the

"Shadows" Portfolio

In addition to writing a cover letter and choosing papers, your portfolio work for *Shadows* includes looking back over the entire first year of your IMP experience.

Cover Letter for "Shadows"

Look back over *Shadows* and describe the central problem of the unit and the main mathematical ideas. This description should give an overview of how the key ideas were developed and how they were used to solve the central problem.

As part of the compilation of your portfolio, you will be selecting some activities that you think were important in developing the key ideas of this unit. Your cover letter should include an explanation of why you select the particular items you do.

Selecting Papers from "Shadows"

Your portfolio for *Shadows* should contain the items described below.

• *Homework 25: Beginning Portfolio Selection*

Include the activities from the unit that you selected in *Homework 25: Beginning Portfolio Selection*, along with your written work about the concept of similarity and about the activities.

Continued on next page

portfolio back tomorrow with the cover letter as the first item. They should also bring any other work that they think will be of help on tomorrow's unit assessments. The remainder of their work can be kept at home.

• **What to do with portfolios?**
We strongly recommend that you keep students' Year 1 portfolios to pass on to their Year 2 teachers. If students have done their portfolio work well, they will find their portfolios to be

- Other key activities

  Include two or three other activities that you think were important in developing the key ideas of this unit.

- A Problem of the Week

  Select one of the four POWs you completed during this unit (*Spiralaterals, Cutting the Pie, Trying Triangles,* and *Pool Pockets*).

- Other quality work

  Select one or two other pieces of work that demonstrate your best efforts. (These can be any work from the unit—Problem of the Week, homework, classwork, presentation, and so forth.)

End-of-Year Review

Because this is the final unit of the year, you should take this chance to look back over your overall experience. Here are some of the issues you might want to examine.

- How was this experience different from your previous work in mathematics

  - in terms of *how* you learned the mathematics?

  - in terms of the mathematics itself?

- How have you changed personally as a result of your experience

  - in terms of your confidence in your own ability?

  - in terms of your work with others?

- What are your mathematics goals for the rest of your high school years? How have those goals changed over the past year and why?

You should include here any other thoughts you might like to share with a reader of your portfolio.

useful assets as they continue through subsequent years of the IMP curriculum.

It may be difficult for the school to store all four years of portfolios, so

you eventually may want to return them to students. This issue is discussed further in the opening unit of Year 2, *Solve It!*

Final Assessments

Students do the in-class assessment and can begin the take-home assessment.

- *In-Class Assessment for "Shadows"*
- *Take-Home Assessment for "Shadows"*

Outline of the Day

In Class

Introduce assessments
- Students do *In-Class Assessment for "Shadows"*
- Students begin *Take-Home Assessment for "Shadows"*

At Home

Students complete *Take-Home Assessment for "Shadows"*

1. End-of-Unit Assessments

Note: The in-class portion of unit assessments is intentionally short so that time pressure will not be a factor in students' ability to do well. The IMP *Teaching Handbook* contains general information about the purpose of end-of-unit assessments and how to use them.

Tell students that today they will get two tests—one that they will finish in class and one that they can start in class and will be able to finish at home. The take-home part should be handed in tomorrow.

Tell students that they are allowed to use graphing calculators, notes from previous work, and so on when they do the assessments. (They will have to do without graphing calculators on the take-home portion unless they have their own.)

These assessments are provided separately in Appendix B for you to duplicate.

In-Class Assessment for "Shadows"

There is a tower of cubes 9 inches tall, placed on a table. You are shining a flashlight at the tower, and the flashlight is mounted on a stand so that it is 24 inches above the tabletop.

The distance from the bottom of the tower to the spot on the table directly below the flashlight is 17 inches.

How long is the shadow cast by the tower? Explain your reasoning.

Take–Home Assessment for *Shadows*

1. *The Ladder*

A ladder is leaning up against a building.

The bottom of the ladder is 3 feet away from the building, and the ladder makes an angle of 75° with the ground.

Answer the following questions and show your work.

    a. How high up on the building does the ladder reach?

    b. How long is the ladder?

Homework:
Complete *Take-Home Assessment for "Shadows"*

Students should bring back the completed assessment tomorrow. As with all work done at home, students may collaborate or get assistance, but they should report this as part of their write-up of the assessment.

2. *Building Measurement*

Find something around your neighborhood that is too tall for you to measure directly, such as the height of your roof or the height of a tree.

    a. Describe in detail *two ways* in which you could find the height of this object *indirectly,* using the ideas you have learned in this unit.

       Be sure to explain why your methods work.

    b. Actually carry out the plan for *one* of your two ways. (You choose which method to use.) Give the specific measurements you make directly, and show how you use those measurements to find the desired height.

Mathematical Topics

• Summarizing the unit

Outline of the Day

1. Discuss unit assessments
2. Sum up the unit

3. Sum up the year

Note: The discussion ideas below are presented as if they take place on the day following the assessments, but you may prefer to delay this material until after you have looked over students' work on the assessments.

These discussion ideas are included here as their own "day" to remind you that some time should be allotted for such a discussion.

1. Discussion of Unit Assessments

You can have students volunteer to explain their work on each of the problems. Encourage questions and alternate explanations from other students.

• In-Class Assessment

You can have one or two students present their work on this problem. The problem should provide a nice summary of some of the main ideas of the central problem of the unit.

• Take-Home Assessment

Question 1 should give you a sense of how well students can handle a straightforward application of trigonometry.

They will probably use a diagram, such as the one below, and see that $\tan 75° = \frac{x}{3}$ and $\cos 75° = \frac{3}{y}$. The first equation gives $x = 3 \tan 75°$, so $x \approx 11.2$ feet. Students may have a little more trouble manipulating the second equation, perhaps getting $y = \frac{3}{\cos 75°} \approx 11.6$ feet.

On Question 2, you will probably get many different approaches, perhaps using shadows, mirrors, angles of elevation, and so on. You can let students share their experiences and techniques, looking for as wide a variety as your students can provide.

2. Unit Summary

Let students share their portfolio cover letters as a way to start a discussion summarizing the unit.

Then let them brainstorm and comment on what they have learned in the unit. This is a good opportunity to review terminology and to place the unit in a broader mathematics context. You may want to emphasize the combination of traditional and nontraditional work that they did in this unit.

3. Summary of the Year

You may want to take some time to have students look over the entire year of mathematics, perhaps asking them to summarize the key concepts that they studied in each unit.

Appendix A
Supplemental Problems

This appendix contains a variety of activities that can be used to supplement the unit material. These activities are included at the end of the student materials and fall roughly into two categories.

- Reinforcements, which are intended to increase students' understanding of and comfort with concepts, techniques, and methods that are discussed in class and that are central to the unit

- Extensions, which allow students to explore ideas beyond the basic unit and which sometimes deal with generalizations or abstractions of ideas that are part of the main unit

The supplemental activities are listed here in the approximate sequence in which they might be used in the unit. (They appear in the same order in the student materials.)

This appendix includes specific recommendations about how each activity might work within the unit.

In addition to the problems listed here, you may want to use supplemental problems from earlier units that were not assigned or not completed. These two supplemental activites may be particularly appropriate:

- *From One to N* (from *Patterns*)

- *Diagonals Illuminated* (from *Patterns*, in relation to ideas of *closed formula* and *recursive function*)

- *Crates* (extension)

  This problem can be used as a follow-up to *Homework 4: An N-by-N Window* and *Homework 5: More About Windows.*

- *Some Other Shadows* (extension)

  This is a very open-ended assignment in which students can investigate other aspects of shadows than those considered in the unit. You can offer it to students any time after they have gotten a clear idea of what the lamp shadow and sun shadow problems are about (for example, after Day 6).

- *Investigation* (extension)

  This activity would be appropriate any time after the initial experimental work and would perhaps be best after the discussion of *Looking for Equations* on Day 6. You may want to give students some time to brainstorm about possible topics. You also may want to let students work in pairs on this project.

- *The Golden Ratio* (extension)

  This activity would probably be meaningful to students once they have started thinking about ratios, so you might use it any time after Day 8 or so. Geometry books and encyclopedias are possible sources of information about the golden ratio (also called the *golden section*). The German psychologist Gustav Fechner (1801–1887), considered the founder of experimental esthetics, wrote about this subject.

- *Rigidity Can Be Good* (extension)

  This problem is appropriate after the students have played with the materials in *Why Are Triangles Special?* on Day 10 and have seen that triangles form rigid structures.

- *Is It Sufficient?* (extension)

  This problem is intended both as a geometric exploration and as a continuation of ideas about logic and counterexamples. It can be used after students have worked on both *Homework 9: Triangular Counterexamples* and *Why Are Triangles Special* (Day 10).

  Students may be perplexed (justifiably) about what it means to say that "a side of one triangle is proportional to a side of the other triangle." If questions come up, help students to articulate the idea that any single number is "proportional to" any other number, so this condition on sides is really not saying anything at all.

- *How Can They Not Be Similar?* (extension)

  This activity continues students' investigation of criteria for similarity, forcing them to look very carefully at the "corresponding parts" aspect of similarity. The problem is quite subtle, and perhaps is best assigned after *Are Angles Enough?* on Day 11.

  The problem will require some ingenuity on the part of students. One method is to start with a quadrilateral that has two equal base angles but is not symmetric, like this:

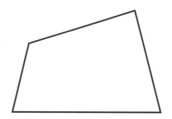

Append to this a non-isosceles triangle with the base of the quadrilateral as one of its sides:

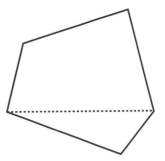

Compare the pentagon above with the pentagon below, which has the triangle reversed.

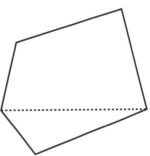

It's not hard to see that the two pentagons have the same set of angles and the same set of lengths of sides, but they are not similar.

- *Triangular Data* (extension)

    You can assign *Triangular Data* after Day 11 to follow up on the ideas in *Why Are Triangles Special?* and *Are Angles Enough?* In *Why Are Triangles Special?* students saw that three lengths determine a triangle. (This is the congruence property traditionally abbreviated as SSS.) This activity provides students with an opportunity to develop the other standard congruence conditions (abbreviated as SAS, ASA, and AAS), and to see that knowing two sides and a nonincluded angle does not necessarily determine a triangle.

- *Scale It!* (reinforcement)

    This is an open-ended activity about scale drawings, and it might be used after *Homework 11: From Top to Bottom,* since that activity refers briefly to scale drawings and students may use ideas about scale drawings in their work on that assignment.

- *Proportions Everywhere* (reinforcement)

    This is a fairly structured activity about proportionality in similar figures, and it can be used after *Homework 11: From Top to Bottom*.

• *What If They Kept Running?* (reinforcement)

This activity asks students to use concepts of proportionality in a context quite different from the geometric work of the unit. You might assign it after either *Homework 10: Similar Problems* or after *Homework 13: Inventing Rules.*

• *Fit Them Together* (extension)

This problem prompts students to begin thinking about the relationship between areas of similar figures, and it might be appropriate after discussion of *Homework 17: Inside Similarity.*

You may choose to get students started with an illustration such as the one below of the special case of squares:

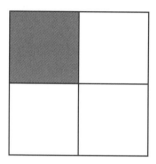

In discussing Question 3, help students to see that, for quadrilaterals where the "fitting together" of Question 2 is possible, the diagram itself is a proof that the area quadruples, so the question has already been answered in such cases. The challenging issue is whether this area relationship holds even when the "fitting together" proof is impossible.

• *Similar Areas* (extension)

This activity is a natural follow-up to the preceding supplemental problem, *Fit Them Together.*

• *The Parallel Postulate* (extension)

This activity offers students an opportunity to learn about the historical background of the parallel postulate. They can work on this any time after Day 15.

• *Exterior Angles and Polygon Angle Sums* (extension)

This activity presents a proof of the angle sum formula for polygons using a method quite different from that in the Day 16 activity, *A Parallel Proof. Exterior Angles and Polygon Angle Sums* makes an excellent follow-up to that other proof.

• *Exactly One-Half!* (extension)

This problem can be used as a follow-up to the discussion of *The Tree and the Pendulum* (Day 23) in which students may notice that sin 30° = 0.5.

- *Eye Exam* (reinforcement)

   This is a fairly routine problem in which students will use trigonometry. *Eye Exam* could be used as an introduction to the idea of inverse trigonometric functions, although students will probably use a guess-and-check approach to finding the given angle.

- *Pole Cat* (reinforcement)

   This is another standard trigonometry problem, although it has some ambiguities (for example, will Wanda Ann jump part way down?) that make it fun.

- *Dog in a Ditch* (reinforcement)

   This looks at first glance like another trigonometry exercise, but in fact, at this stage probably the only way for students to solve this problem is through the use of a scale drawing. (The law of sines provides the simplest solution, but students won't learn about that until Year 4.)

Supplemental Problems

Many of the supplemental problems for *Shadows* focus on similarity, but other problems look at logic and counterexamples, at the use of proportions, or at the history underlying concepts from the unit. These are some examples.

This page in the student book introduces the supplemental problems

- *Fit Them Together* and *Similar Areas* examine the connection between area and similarity.

- *Is It Sufficient?* and *Triangular Data* look at the conditions needed for similarity and congruence, and ask you to find counterexamples or generalizations.

- *Proportions Everywhere* uses proportionality in a geometric setting. *What If They Kept Running?* looks at proportionality in the context of a track competition.

- *The Parallel Postulate* gives you a glimpse into the historical development of ideas about parallelism. Reading on your own, you'll learn how these ideas led to the development of non-Euclidean geometry.

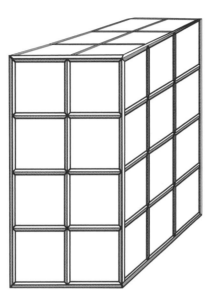

In *Homework 4: An N-by-N Window* and in *Homework 5: More About Windows,* you looked for formulas for the amount of wood strip needed to create a window frame.

Now suppose that instead of building a window frame, you are building a frame for a wooden crate, such as the one shown at the left.

Keep in mind that the wood strip is just used to make a *frame* for the crate. Cardboard has been placed between the strips to make the crate into a solid box.

Because of the cardboard, you can't see the bottom or the back sides of the crate in the diagram.

1. First find the amount of wood strip needed if the crate is 2 feet wide, 3 feet long, and 4 feet high, as shown above.

   Remember that only three sides of the crate are shown here, so you'll need to imagine the other three sides. Also remember that some of the wood strips are shared by two sides of the crate.

2. Now look for a general formula, using a crate that is *w* feet wide, *l* feet long, and *h* feet high.

Some Other Shadows

The central problem in this unit involves finding the length of a shadow cast on the floor by a lamp or streetlight.

But what if the shadow is cast along a surface that isn't horizontal? For example, the picture below shows someone using a lamp to create shadows on a wall.

These other kinds of shadows may be difficult to study, but give it a try. You don't have to look at the length of the shadow—you can investigate any aspect you like.

Investigation

In *The Pit and the Pendulum,* you experimented with pendulums of different weights to see if changing the weight of the bob caused a change in the length of the pendulum's period.

In this unit, you began by experimenting with shadows, studying how changing certain lengths or distances affected the length of the shadow.

In each of these investigations, it was important that everything was the same in each experiment except for the variable you were testing. In other words, each experiment had one variable (such as the weight of the bob) that you were changing, and one result (such as the length of the period) that you looked at to see if there was an effect.

For this assignment, you are to think of your own topic of investigation. In your investigation, as before, there should be one variable that changes (the **independent variable**) and one result (the **dependent variable**) where you look for an effect.

You are to create an experiment on your topic that will provide data for you to analyze. Your goal is to come up with some kind of formula that will describe your data. (There may not be an exact formula. In that case, you should either look for an approximate formula or come up with a verbal description of what is happening.)

Continued on next page

Here is a suggested plan:

1. Decide on a topic to investigate. You should pick a topic that can be organized so that there is one independent variable and one dependent variable. Everything else should remain constant.

2. Design the experiment.

3. Do one or two trial runs of your experiment and refine it as necessary.

4. Collect and organize the data.

5. Try to use your data to come up with a formula or verbal description of what is happening.

You will need to turn in a summary of your work. You can use the steps above as an outline.

The Golden Ratio

There is a ratio that often comes up in art and nature called the **golden ratio** (or the **golden section**). Many people think that structures that make use of this ratio are visually appealing.

Research the golden ratio and write a paper on what it is and where it occurs. The paper should be at least two pages in length and should include a list of the sources of your information.

Rigidity Can Be Good

You saw in *Why Are Triangles Special?* that if you "build" a triangle using specific lengths for the sides, then the triangle is *rigid*. That is, once the sides are put together, there is no flexibility.

For polygons with more than three sides, though, the polygon can be "flexed" at the corners, which changes the shape without changing the lengths of the sides.

Of course, in many situations, it's important to be flexible. But in architecture, it can be important that a building keep its shape.

Investigate the significance of rigidity for architecture and construction. You may want to do some construction of your own, or you may want to read about how triangles can be used to make buildings stable.

Suggestion: Look up the work of R. Buckminster Fuller.

Is It Sufficient?

As you already know, you can conclude that two triangles are similar whenever you know that two angles of one triangle are equal to two angles of the other triangle.

Mathematicians express this by saying that having two pairs of equal angles is **sufficient** for concluding that two triangles are similar.

Your goal in this problem is to investigate what other information about two triangles can be considered sufficient to conclude that the triangles are similar.

For each of the conditions stated below, start out as a skeptic. Use your ruler and

Continued on next page

protractor to make sketches, and try to find two triangles that fit the condition but that *are not* similar. In other words, look for a counterexample. If you find such triangles, you will have shown that the particular combination is not sufficient to conclude that the triangles are similar.

On the other hand, you may decide a given condition *is* sufficient; that is, that there are no counterexamples. In that case, try to explain why any two triangles that fit the condition must be similar.

Condition 1

An angle of one triangle is equal to an angle of the other triangle.

Condition 2

A side of one triangle is proportional to a side of the other triangle.

Condition 3

A pair of sides of one triangle is proportional to a pair of sides of the other triangle.

Condition 4

The three sides of one triangle are proportional to the three sides of the other triangle.

Condition 5

An angle of one triangle is equal to an angle of the other triangle, and a side of one triangle is proportional to a side of the other triangle.

Condition 6

A pair of sides of one triangle is proportional to a pair of sides of the other triangle, and the angles between these pairs of sides are equal.

Condition 7

A pair of sides of one triangle is proportional to a pair of sides of the other triangle, and an angle not between the pair in one triangle is equal to the corresponding angle of the other triangle.

How Can They Not Be Similar?

You know that two polygons are similar if they satisfy both of these conditions.

- The angles of the first polygon are equal to the corresponding angles of the second.

- The sides of the first polygon are proportional to the corresponding sides of the second.

But what if the word "corresponding" is omitted? Do the polygons still have to be similar?

The answer is no, but constructing a counterexample is not easy. To make life simpler for you, look at the special case where the ratio of sides is 1.

In other words, your task in this activity is to try to construct two polygons that satisfy both of the following conditions but that are not similar.

- The angles of the first are equal (as a group) to the angles of the second.

- The lengths of the sides of the first polygon are equal (as a group) to the lengths of the sides of the second.

Triangular Data

You saw in *Why Are Triangles Special?* that if you were given three lengths, there would be at most one way to build a triangle whose sides had those lengths.

Mathematicians express this property by saying that the lengths of the sides **determine** the triangle.

Here's another way to express this property.

> *If the sides of one triangle have the same lengths as the sides of another triangle, then the two triangles must be congruent.*

We sometimes think of a triangle as having six parts—three sides and three angles. As just discussed, three sides determine a triangle. You saw in *Are Angles Enough?* that three angles do *not* determine a triangle, since two triangles with the same angles might be similar but not congruent.

In Part I of this activity, you will explore through examples what other combinations of information determine a triangle. In Part II, you will try to generalize your discoveries.

Continued on next page

Part I: Exploring Triangles

In each of the problems below, you are given the values for three of the six parts of a possible triangle, $\triangle ABC$. You are to try to draw a triangle that fits the conditions. In each case you have to answer two questions:

        a. Is it possible to draw a triangle that fits the conditions?

        b. If so, will two triangles that both fit the conditions have to be congruent to each other?

In other words, your task is to find out if the given information determines a triangle.

Each of Questions 1 through 8 is a separate problem. Answer both part a and part b for each example and justify your answers.

Note: You will probably find it helpful to use a ruler and a protractor on this assignment.

    1. $AC = 5$ inches, $\angle ABC = 50°$, and $\angle CAB = 110°$

    2. $BC = 7$ inches, $\angle ABC = 70°$, and $\angle BCA = 80°$

    3. $AB = 5$ inches, $BC = 8$ inches, and $\angle ABC = 70°$

    4. $AB = 7$ inches, $AC = 11$ inches, and $\angle CAB = 130°$

    5. $AB = 7$ inches, $AC = 6$ inches, and $\angle ABC = 50°$

    6. $AB = 2$ inches, $BC = 4$ inches, and $\angle BCA = 60°$

    7. $AB = 3$ inches, $AC = 5$ inches, and $\angle ABC = 90°$

    8. $AB = 4$ inches, $BC = 6$ inches, and $\angle CAB = 100°$

Part II: Generalizing Triangles

Look at the examples above, and consider these questions.

    • How many lengths and how many angles were provided in each case?

    • How were the lengths and angles situated in relation to each other in the triangle?

Based on these examples and others you might create on your own, try to develop some general principles. The central question to explore is

    What type of information determines a triangle?

Scale It!

Scale drawings and scale models are used for many purposes, such as map-making and testing new inventions.

Here are a few options you might consider for an investigation of scaling.

- Make a scale drawing of some aspect of your school or neighborhood.

- Build a scale model of some object.

- Interview someone who uses scale drawings or scale models in his or her work.

If you have other ideas for learning more about scaling, that's fine too.

Whatever you do, write a report about your work and discuss how the ideas of this unit were connected to your investigation.

Proportions Everywhere

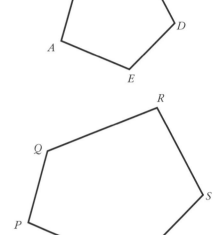

Polygons *ABCDE* and *PQRST* at the right are similar, so the ratios of the lengths of corresponding sides are the same.

For example, the ratio $\frac{AB}{PQ}$ is the same as the ratio $\frac{CD}{RS}$, because $\overline{AB}$ corresponds to $\overline{PQ}$ and $\overline{CD}$ corresponds to $\overline{RS}$.

What about other lengths in these diagrams? Does every part of the first figure have a corresponding part in the second? Do other ratios of corresponding parts come out the same as the ratios above? First look at some examples.

1. Consider the diagonal $\overline{BE}$ in the first polygon.

   a. What segment in the second polygon corresponds to this diagonal?

   b. Is the ratio of the length of $\overline{BE}$ to the length of its corresponding part the same as the ratio of *AB* to *PQ?* Why or why not?

2. Use *F* to represent the midpoint of side $\overline{AE}$.

   a. What segment in the second polygon corresponds to $\overline{CF}$?

   b. Is the ratio of the length of $\overline{CF}$ to the length of its corresponding part the same as the ratio of *AB* to *PQ*? Why or why not?

Now make up your own examples and think about generalizing. State clearly any general principles you think must hold true.

What If They Kept Running?

Mandy, Callie, and Kate were running a race of 1500 meters. Mandy won.

At the moment when Mandy crossed the finish line, she was 300 meters ahead of Callie and 420 meters ahead of Kate.

If Callie and Kate keep running at the same rates as they have run so far, how many meters ahead of Kate will Callie be when Callie crosses the finish line?

Adapted from *Mathematics Teacher* (January 1990), National Council of Teachers of Mathematics, Volume 83, Number 1.

Fit Them Together

The illustration below shows how to start with one triangle (the top triangle) and fit four copies of it together to make a "double-size" version of that triangle.

Such a diagram shows that the large triangle is similar to the original triangle, because each side is twice as long. The diagram also shows that the area of the "double-size" triangle is four times the area of the original triangle.

1. Can you do this "fitting together" starting with any triangle? Try either to find a triangle for which you can't put four copies together this way, or to explain why this diagram works for any initial triangle.

2. Now move on to quadrilaterals. If you start with any initial quadrilateral, can you fit four exact copies of it together to make a "double-size" version of that quadrilateral?

   This may depend on the initial quadrilateral. Start with squares, then move on to rectangles, parallelograms, trapezoids, and others. In each case, explore whether four exact copies can be put together to make a "double-size" version.

   If you think that this can be done with a given category of quadrilaterals, show how. If you find quadrilaterals for which this "fitting together" cannot be done, show some of them.

3. That still leaves a question about area. If you start with an arbitrary quadrilateral and make a similar quadrilateral whose sides are twice as long as those of the original, will the area of this "double-size" quadrilateral always be four times the area of the original?

   Either explain why this is so, or give a counterexample.

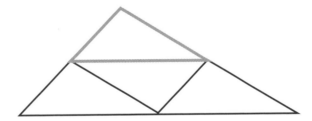

492

Similar Areas

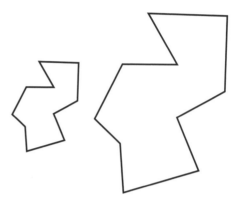

In *Fit Them Together,* you saw that you could double the lengths of the sides of a triangle to create a new triangle that was similar to the original and that had an area four times that of the original.

What more can you say about areas of similar figures?

Specifically, how does the ratio of the area of two similar figures depend on the ratio of the lengths of corresponding sides?

The Parallel Postulate

When the Greek mathematician Euclid wrote his *Elements* (about 300 B.C.E.), he made certain fundamental geometric assumptions, called **postulates** and **axioms**.

For example, his first postulate says

> A straight line may be drawn between any two points.

That's pretty reasonable. Most of his postulates are just as simple as this first one.

But Euclid's fifth postulate is quite complicated. It says

> If two straight lines lying in a plane are met by another line, and if the sum of the interior angles on one side is less than two right angles, then the straight lines if extended sufficiently will meet on the side on which the sum of the angles is less than two right angles.

1. What does this mean? Draw a diagram to explain what Euclid was talking about. (*Hint:* The phrase "another line" corresponds to what was called a *transversal* in the activity *More About Angles.* In other words, this line crosses each of the other two lines.)

2. Explain how this postulate is related to the principles about parallel lines that you found in *More About Angles.* In particular, discuss the connection between Euclid's fifth postulate and the statement

> Given a line L and a point P not on L, there is a unique line through P that is parallel to L.

This statement is sometimes called **Playfair's axiom**, after the Scottish mathematician John Playfair (1748-1819).

Mathematicians were intrigued by Euclid's fifth postulate, partly because it was so complicated. A long history developed in which they tried to prove this statement without making any assumptions except for Euclid's other postulates. They were never successful.

In the nineteenth century, three mathematicians in three different countries showed that this challenge was impossible. A German mathematician, Carl Friedrich Gauss (1777-1855), a Russian mathematician, Nicolai Ivanovitch Lobachevsky (1793-1856), and a Hungarian mathematician, Janós Bolyai (1802-1860), all explored the idea of a geometric system in which Euclid's postulate was false. Quite independently of each

Continued on next page

other, they discovered that such a system was logically possible. The system they developed is called **hyperbolic geometry**.

Another geometric system, which required changing some of Euclid's other postulates, was developed by the German mathematician Georg Friedrich Bernhard Riemann (1826–1866), and this is called **elliptic geometry**.

Both are examples of geometrical systems that describe the geometry of surfaces other than a plane, and both are examples of a broader field called **non-Euclidean geometry**. It turns out that Albert Einstein made use of the ideas of non-Euclidean geometry in developing his concepts of space and time that are part of the theory of relativity.

3. Read about and report further on the history of Euclid's fifth postulate and the development of non-Euclidean geometry.

Exterior Angles and Polygon Angle Sums

In *A Parallel Proof,* you saw how to use principles about parallel lines to prove that the sum of the angles of any triangle is exactly 180°. You also know that this fact for triangles can be used to develop an angle sum formula for arbitrary polygons. It turns out that these facts about angle sums can also be proved by using a concept called **exterior angles.**

This activity will explain that concept and then give a sequence of questions to help you develop that proof.

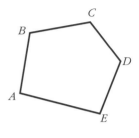

Exterior Angles

Generally, when we talk about the angles of a polygon, we mean the angles *inside* the figure. For example, in the first pentagon, we might mean ∠*ABC* or ∠*DEA,* among others.

But you get some other interesting angles by extending the sides of the polygon. For example, the diagram at the right shows the same polygon with $\overline{BC}$ extended beyond *C* to point *F*.

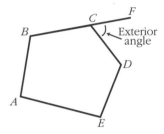

The angle *FCD* is called an **exterior angle** of the polygon. For emphasis, we sometimes call an angle inside a polygon, such as ∠*BCD,* an **interior angle.**

There are actually two exterior angles at each vertex of a polygon. For example, at *C,* in addition to extending $\overline{BC}$ as above, you could also extend $\overline{DC}$ past *C,* as shown at the right. Both ∠*BCK* and ∠*FCD* are considered exterior angles at *C* for polygon *ABCDE.*

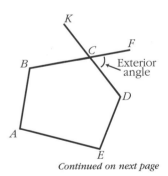

In this activity, you will only be considering one exterior angle at each vertex.

Note: Since angles *FCD* and *BCK* are vertical angles, they are equal, and it won't matter which one is used.

Continued on next page

496   Interactive Mathematics Program

Polygon Angle Sums

The proof of the angle sum formula for polygons combines two ideas:

- The relationship between each interior angle and the corresponding exterior angle

- A general formula about exterior angles

In this activity, you will develop the two ideas separately and then put them together.

Step 1. Interior and Exterior Angles

Step 1 is the easier of the two parts, and it has two stages. First you need to answer this question.

> *What is the relationship between an interior angle of a polygon and the corresponding exterior angle?*

For example, how are angles *BCD* and *FCD* related?

Write a formula or equation relating two such angles, and explain why that relationship must hold for every such pair of angles.

Your answer to the question above should give you a formula for the sum of each interior angle and the corresponding exterior angle. Basing your response on that result, answer this question.

> *If you combine all the interior angles with their corresponding exterior angles (using only one exterior angle for each vertex), what is the sum of all of these angles?*

Hint: The answer depends on the number of sides of the polygon.

Step 2. Total Turns

The second key idea involves just the exterior angles of a polygon, choosing one at each vertex, as shown in the diagram at the right.

Imagine that you are standing at point *C*, facing toward *F*. From that position, turn toward *D,* turning through an angle equal to the exterior angle *FCD*.

Now move along $\overline{CD}$ to point *D*. When you get there, turn toward *E*, this time turning through an angle equal to exterior angle *JDE*.

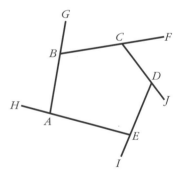

Continued on next page

Next, move along $\overline{DE}$ to E, and again make a turn. Continue around the polygon in this way, moving along each side and then turning through the exterior angle.

Your final turn will occur when you are at point B, facing toward G. You will turn toward C, going through a turn equal to the last of the exterior angles. You are now facing in the same direction in which you started.

The key question here is

What is the total number of degrees in all of your turns?

In other words, what is the sum of all the exterior angles of the polygon (taking one exterior angle at each vertex)?

Would your result work for any polygon? Explain.

Step 3. Putting It All Together

In Step 1, you should have found a formula for the sum of an interior angle and its corresponding exterior angle, and from that you should have found a formula for the sum of all the interior and exterior angles.

In Step 2, you should have found a formula for the sum of all the exterior angles.

The final step of the process is

What is the sum of the interior angles of the polygon?

Exactly One-Half!

You may have observed that, according to your calculator, sin 30° = 0.5000.

You might wonder whether this is just an approximation or if sin 30° is really *exactly* one-half.

Your task in this activity is to show, beyond any doubt, that the sine of 30° is exactly, precisely one-half.

Hint: Use an equilateral triangle and the fact that the sum of the angles of a triangle is 180°.

Eye Exam

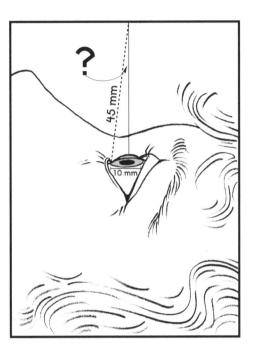

An eye surgeon must perform an operation on a person who has pressure behind the cornea. (The cornea is the shaded area in the picture.) The surgeon will use a laser to make small holes along the edge of the cornea.

The patient will be lying on the operating table and the laser will be above her. More precisely, it will be directly above her pupil (the center of her eye). The laser is 45 millimeters from the outer edge of the cornea. The diameter of the cornea is 10 millimeters.

The surgeon needs to find the angle at which to set the laser. This is the angle shown in the diagram as "?"

1. Using trigonometry, set up an equation that could be used to find this angle.

2. Use your scientific calculator to get an approximate solution to this equation (by trial and error).

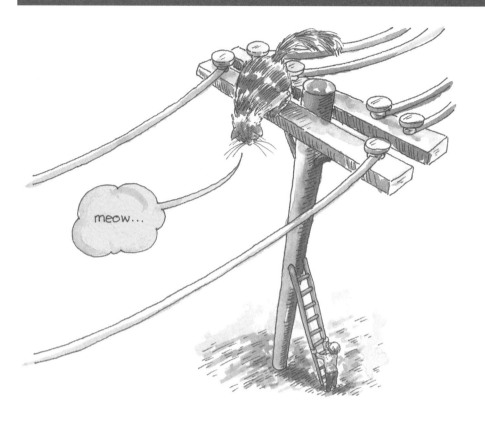

Pole Cat

Poor Diane. Her cat, Wanda Ann, has climbed up a telephone pole and can't get down.

The crossbar of the telephone pole is 20 feet high. Diane is 5 feet 6 inches tall and can reach a foot above her head. She has a 15-foot ladder.

In order to keep the ladder from tipping, Diane must lean it against the pole at an angle of 70° with the ground. Can Diane save Wanda Ann?

Dog in a Ditch

Oscar and Rasheed are identical twins. They are both 6 feet tall. They are on opposite sides of a ditch that is 30 feet wide. Their dog, Earl, is at the bottom of the ditch.

Earl can get out if he wants to. When Oscar looks at Earl, his line of sight makes a 75° angle below the horizontal. When Rasheed looks at Earl, his line of sight makes a 40° angle below horizontal. How deep is the ditch?

(*Hint:* Trigonometry may not be very useful in this problem.)

Appendix B
Blackline Masters

This appendix contains copies of the in-class and take-home assessments for the unit.

This appendix also contains a suggested second semester final assessment for classes on a traditional semester schedule. The assessment is designed on the assumption that by the end of the second semester your class will have completed the third unit of the year, *The Overland Trail,* as well as the fourth and fifth units, *The Pit and the Pendulum* and *Shadows.* This assessment is not intended to be a comprehensive test of the material in these units, but focuses instead on some essential ideas.

We recommend that you give students two hours for this assessment so they can complete it without time pressure, and that you allow them to use graphing calculators and to have access to their textbooks and notes (including portfolios).

In-Class Assessment for "Shadows"

There is a tower of cubes 9 inches tall, placed on a table. You are shining a flashlight at the tower, and the flashlight is mounted on a stand so that it is 24 inches above the tabletop.

The distance from the bottom of the tower to the spot on the table directly below the flashlight is 17 inches.

How long is the shadow cast by the tower? Explain your reasoning.

Take-Home Assessment for *Shadows*

1. *The Ladder*

A ladder is leaning up against a building.

The bottom of the ladder is 3 feet away from the building, and the ladder makes an angle of 75° with the ground.

Answer the following questions and show your work.

    a. How high up on the building does the ladder reach?

    b. How long is the ladder?

2. *Building Measurement*

Find something around your neighborhood that is too tall for you to measure directly, such as the height of your roof or the height of a tree.

a. Describe in detail *two ways* in which you could find the height of this object *indirectly,* using the ideas you have learned in this unit.

Be sure to explain why your methods work.

b. Actually carry out the plan for *one* of your two ways. (You choose which method to use.) Give the specific measurements you make directly, and show how you use those measurements to find the desired height.

I. *What's It All About?*

For this problem, choose *two* of these three concepts:

    a. similarity of polygons

    b. standard deviation

    c. In-Out table

Follow these steps for *each* of your *two* choices:

- Explain what the concept means.

- Describe a situation in which the concept could be used.

- Give an example of a question that might arise in the situation you described that the concept would help to answer.

- Show the calculations that you would need to make to answer the question. Make up sample numbers to illustrate how to do this.

II. *The Telephone Decision*

Two new telephone companies—Ding-a-Ling Telephone and Beep Beep Telephone—are trying to enter the local market. Here are the prices for their services:

Ding-a-Ling Telephone

$5.00   base fee per month

$0.10   for each local call

Beep Beep Telephone

$8.00   base fee per month

$0.06   for each local call

1. a. The Strand family makes about 85 local calls per month. Which service is better for them? Why?

   b. The Marino family makes about 60 local calls per month. Which service is better for them? Why?

2. a. Make an In-Out table that the Ding-a-Ling Telephone Company could use to give advice to consumers, which compares the number of calls with the corresponding cost.

   b. Write a rule to describe the relationship in your table.

   c. Make a graph from this information.

3. a. Make an In-Out table that the Beep Beep Telephone Company could use to give advice to consumers, which compares the number of calls with the corresponding cost.

   b. Write a rule to describe the relationship in this table.

   c. On the same set of axes that you used to make the graph for the Ding-a-Ling Telephone Company, now make a graph for the Beep Beep Telephone Company.

4. Which service would be better for your own family and why?

5. Imagine that you represent a consumer group in your neighborhood. You are responsible for advising new people who move into the area which telephone company would best suit their needs. What would you tell people about choosing a telephone company? Why?

III. Boingggg!!!!!

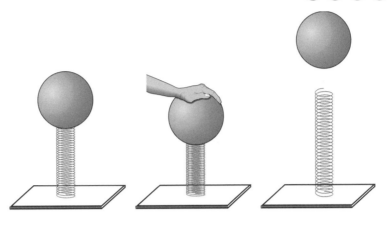

Students in a science class were studying how springs behave. They mounted a large spring on a table, and rested a ball on top of the spring. Then they pushed the ball down. As they did so, they tightened, or *compressed,* the spring. When they let go, the ball was shot into the air (to no one's surprise).

They did experiments in which they varied how far down they pushed the ball (called the *amount of compression*), and then they measured how high the ball went, compared to its resting position, as carefully as they could. They got the following data:

Amount of compression (in cm)	Height the ball rises from resting point (in cm)
3	10
5	30
8	70
10	110

1. Make a graph of this information.
2. Use any methods you think are appropriate to get a rule describing how the height depends on the amount of compression. Describe your method and give your results clearly.
3. Make a prediction about how high the ball would go above its resting position if the spring were compressed 15 cm. Explain carefully how you reached your prediction.
4. List other variables that might affect the height a ball goes up from a spring. Describe what experiments you could do to study the effects of these other variables.

IV. Mini-POW

Solve this problem. Then write up your results in POW style, describing your process, your solution, and any extensions or generalizations.

Matt ate a total of 100 raisins over a five-day period. After the first day, he ate six more raisins each day than on the previous day. How many raisins did he eat the first day?

Glossary

This is the glossary for all five units of IMP Year 1.

Absolute value   The distance a number is from 0 on the number line. The symbol | | stands for absolute value.

Examples: $|-2| = 2$; $|7| = 7$; $|0| = 0$

Acute angle   An angle that measures more than $0°$ and less than $90°$.

Acute triangle   A triangle whose angles are all acute.

Adjacent angles   Two angles with the same vertex and formed using a shared ray.

Example: Angles *A* and *B* are adjacent angles.

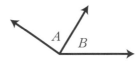

Adjacent side   (for an acute angle of a right triangle) The side of the right triangle which, together with the hypotenuse, forms the given angle.

Example: In the right triangle *ABC*, side $\overline{BC}$ is adjacent to $\angle C$, and side $\overline{AB}$ is adjacent to $\angle A$.

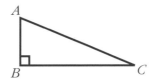

Alternate interior angles   If two lines are intersected by a transversal, then the inside angles that are on opposite sides of the transversal are alternate interior angles.

Example: Angles *K* and *L* are one pair of alternate interior angles, and angles *M* and *N* are another pair.

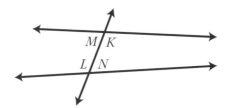

Amplitude   (for a pendulum) The angle of a pendulum's swing, measured from the vertical to the most outward position of the pendulum during its swing.

Example: The pendulum in the diagram has an amplitude of 20°.

Angle   Informally, an amount of turn, usually measured in **degrees.** Formally, the geometric figure formed by two **rays** with a common initial point, called the **vertex** of the angle.

Angle of elevation   The angle at which an object appears above the horizontal, as measured from a chosen point.

Example: The diagram shows the angle of elevation to the top of the tree from point *A*.

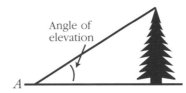

Area   Informally, the amount of space inside a two-dimensional figure, usually measured in square units.

Area model   For probability, a diagram showing the possible outcomes of a particular event. Each portion of the model represents an outcome, and the ratio of the area of that portion to the area of the whole model is the probability of that outcome.

Axis	(plural: **axes**) See **Coordinate system.**
Coefficient	Usually, a number being used to multiply a variable or power of a variable in an algebraic expression. Example: In the expression $3x + 4x^2$, 3 and 4 are coefficients.
Complementary angles	A pair of angles whose measures add to 90°. If two complementary angles are adjacent, together they form a right angle.
Composite number	A counting number having more than two whole-number divisors. Example: 12 is a composite number because it has the divisors 1, 2, 3, 4, 6, and 12.
Conclusion	Informally, any statement arrived at by reasoning or through examples. See also **"If . . . , then . . ." statement.**
Conditional probability	The probability that an event will occur based on the assumption that some other event has already occurred.
Congruent	Informally, having the same shape and size. Formally, two polygons are congruent if their corresponding angles have equal measure and their corresponding sides are equal in length. The symbol ≅ means "is congruent to."
Conjecture	A theory or an idea about how something works, usually based on examples.
Constraint	Informally, a limitation or restriction.
Continuous graph	Informally, a graph that can be drawn without lifting the pencil, in contrast to a **discrete graph.**
Coordinate system	A way to represent points in the plane with pairs of numbers called **coordinates.** The system is based on

two perpendicular lines, one horizontal and one vertical, called **coordinate axes.** The point where the lines meet is called the **origin.** Traditionally, the axes are labeled with the variables x and y as shown below. The horizontal axis is often called the **x-axis** and the vertical axis is often called the **y-axis.**

Example: Point A has coordinates $(3, -2)$.

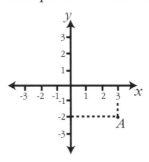

Corresponding angles

(for a transversal) If two lines are intersected by a transversal, then two angles are corresponding angles if they occupy the same position relative to the transversal and the other lines that form them.

Example: Angles A and D are a pair of corresponding angles, and angles B and E are another pair of corresponding angles.

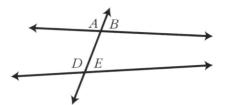

Corresponding parts

For a pair of similar or congruent polygons, sides or angles of the two polygons that have the same relative position.

Example: Side a in the small triangle and side b in the large triangle are corresponding parts.

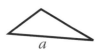 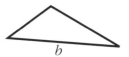

Counterexample	An example which demonstrates that a conjecture is not true.
Degree	The measurement unit for an angle defined by having a complete turn equal to 360 degrees. The symbol ° represents degrees.
Diagonal	In a polygon, a line segment that connects two vertices and that is not a side of the polygon.
Discrete graph	A graph consisting of isolated or unconnected points, in contrast to a **continuous graph.**
Divisor	A factor of an integer. Example: 1, 2, 3, 4, 6, and 12 are the positive divisors of 12.
Domain	The set of values that can be used as inputs for a given function.
Equilateral triangle	A triangle with all sides the same length.
Expected value	In a game or other probability situation, the average amount gained or lost per turn in the long run.
Exterior angle	An angle formed outside a polygon by extending one of its sides. Example: The diagram shows an exterior angle for polygon *ABCDE*. 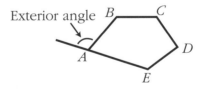
Factor	The same as **divisor.**
Factorial	The product of all the whole numbers from a particular number down to 1. The symbol ! stands for factorial. Example: 5! (read "five factorial") means 5 · 4 · 3 · 2 · 1.
Fair game	A game in which both players are expected to come out equally well in the long run.

Frequency bar graph	A bar graph showing how often each result occurs.

Example: This frequency bar graph shows, for instance, that 11 times in 80 rolls, the sum of two dice was 6.

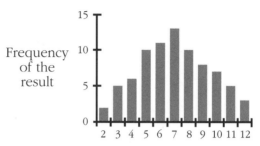

Function	Informally, a process or rule for determining the numerical value of one variable in terms of another. A function is often represented as a set of number pairs in which the second number is determined by the first, according to the function rule.
Graph	A mathematical diagram for displaying information.
Hexagon	A polygon with six sides.
Hypotenuse	The longest side in a right triangle, or the length of this side. The hypotenuse is located opposite the right angle.

Example: In right triangle *ABC*, the hypotenuse is $\overline{AC}$.

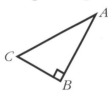

Hypothesis	Informally, a theory about a situation or about how a certain set of data is behaving. Also, a set of assumptions being used to analyze or understand a situation.

See also **"If . . . , then . . ." statement.**

"If . . . , then . . ." statement	A specific form of mathematical statement, saying that if one condition is true, then another condition must also be true.

Example: Here is a true "If . . . , then . . ." statement.

If two angles of a triangle have equal measure, then the sides opposite these angles have equal length.

The condition "two angles of a triangle have equal measure" is the **hypothesis.** The condition "the sides opposite these angles have equal length" is the **conclusion.**

Independent events

Two (or more) events are independent if the outcome of one does not influence the outcome of the other.

Integer

Any number that is either a counting number, zero, or the opposite of a counting number. The integers can be represented using set notation as

$$\{ \ldots -3, -2, -1, 0, 1, 2, 3, \ldots \}$$

Examples: $-4, 0,$ and 10 are integers.

Interior angle

An angle inside a figure, especially within a polygon.

Example: Angle *BAE* is an interior angle of the polygon *ABCDE*.

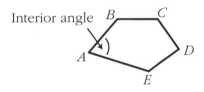

Isosceles triangle

A triangle with two sides of equal length.

Leg

Either of the two shorter sides in a right triangle. The two legs of a right triangle form the right angle of the triangle. The longest side of a right triangle (the hypotenuse) is not considered a leg.

Line of best fit

Informally, the line that comes closest to fitting a given set of points on a discrete graph.

Line segment

The portion of a straight line between two given points.

Mathematical model

A mathematical description or structure used to represent how a real-life situation works.

Mean

The numerical average of a data set, found by adding the data items and dividing by the number of items in the set.

Example: For the data set 8, 12, 12, 13, and 17, the sum of the data items is 62 and there are 5 items in the data set, so the mean is 62 ÷ 5, or 12.4.

Measurement variation   The situation of taking several measurements of the same thing and getting different results.

Median   (of a set of data) The "middle number" in a set of data that has been arranged from smallest to largest.

Example: For the data set 4, 17, 22, 56, and 100, the median is 22, because it is the number in the middle of the list.

Mode   (of a set of data) The number that occurs most often in a set of data. Many sets of data do not have a single mode.

Example: For the data set 3, 4, 7, 16, 18, 18, and 23, the mode is 18.

Natural number   Any of the counting numbers 1, 2, 3, 4, and so on.

Normal distribution   A certain precisely defined set of probabilities, which can often be used to approximate real-life events. Sometimes used to refer to any data set whose frequency bar graph is approximately "bell-shaped."

Observed probability   The likelihood of a certain event happening based on observed results, as distinct from **theoretical probability.**

Obtuse angle   An angle that measures more than 90° and less than 180°.

Obtuse triangle   A triangle with an obtuse angle.

Octagon   An eight-sided polygon.

Opposite side   The side of a triangle across from a given angle.

Order of operations   A set of conventions that mathematicians have agreed to use whenever a calculation involves more than one operation.

Example: 2 + 3 · 4 is 14, not 20, because the conventions for order of operations tell us to multiply before we add.

Ordered pair	Two numbers paired together using the format *(x, y)*, often used to locate a point in the coordinate system.
Origin	See **Coordinate system.**
Parallel lines	Two lines in a plane that do not intersect.
Pentagon	A five-sided polygon.
Perimeter	The boundary of a polygon, or the total length of this boundary.
Period	The length of time for a cyclical event to complete one full cycle.
Perpendicular lines	A pair of lines that form a right angle.
Polygon	A closed two-dimensional shape formed by three or more line segments. The line segments that form a polygon are called its sides. The endpoints of these segments are called **vertices** (singular: **vertex**).

Examples: All the figures below are polygons.

Prime number	A whole number greater than 1 that has only two whole number divisors, 1 and itself.

Example: 7 is a prime number, because its only whole number divisors are 1 and 7.

Probability	The likelihood of a certain event happening. For a situation involving equally likely outcomes, the probability that the outcome of an event will be an outcome within a given set is defined by a ratio:

$$\text{Probability} = \frac{\text{number of outcomes in the set}}{\text{total number of possible outcomes}}$$

Example: If a die has 2 red faces and 4 green faces, the probability of getting a green face is

$$\frac{\text{number of green faces}}{\text{total number of faces}} = \frac{4}{6}$$

Proof An absolutely convincing argument.

Proportion A statement that two ratios are equal.

Proportional Having the same ratio.

Example: Corresponding sides of triangles *ABC* and *DEF* are proportional, because the ratios $\frac{4}{6}$, $\frac{8}{12}$, and $\frac{10}{15}$ are equal.

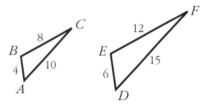

Quadrant One of the four areas created in a coordinate system by using the *x*-axis and the *y*-axis as boundaries. The quadrants have standard numbering as shown below.

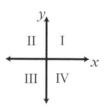

Quadrilateral A four-sided polygon.

Random Used in probability to indicate that any of several events is equally likely or that an event is selected from a set of events according to a precisely described distribution.

Range (of a set of data) The difference between the largest and smallest numbers in the set.

Example: For the data set 7, 12, 18, 18, and 29, the range is 29 – 7, or 22.

Ray The part of a line from a single point, called the **vertex,** through another point on the line and continuing infinitely in that direction.

Rectangle	A four-sided polygon whose angles are all right angles.
Regular polygon	A polygon whose sides all have equal length and whose angles all have equal measure.
Rhombus	A four-sided polygon whose sides all have the same length.
Right angle	An angle that measures 90°.
Right triangle	A triangle with a right angle.
Sample standard deviation	The calculation on a set of data taken from a larger population of data, used to estimate the standard deviation of the larger population.
Sequence	A list of numbers or expressions, usually following a pattern or rule.

Example: 1, 3, 5, 7, 9, . . . is the sequence of positive odd numbers. |
Similar	Informally, having the same shape. Formally, two polygons are similar if their corresponding angles have equal measure and their corresponding sides are proportional in length. The symbol ~ means "is similar to."
Simulation	An experiment or set of experiments using a model of a certain event that is based on the same probabilities as the real event. Simulations allow people to estimate the likelihood of an event when it is impractical to experiment with the real event.
Slope	Informally, the steepness of a line.
Solution	A number that, when substituted for a variable in an equation, makes the equation a true statement.

Example: The value $x = 3$ is a solution to the equation $2x = 6$ because $2 \cdot 3 = 6$. |
| *Square* | A four-sided polygon with all sides of equal length and with four right angles. |

Square root	A number whose square is a given number. The symbol $\sqrt{}$ is used to denote the nonnegative square root of a number.
	Example: Both 6 and –6 are square roots of 36, because $6^2 = 36$ and $(-6)^2 = 36$; $\sqrt{36} = 6$.
Standard deviation	A specific measurement of how spread out a set of data is, usually represented by the lowercase Greek letter sigma (σ).
Straight angle	An angle that measures 180°. The rays forming a straight angle together make up a straight line.
Strategy	A complete plan about how to proceed in a game or problem situation. A strategy for a game should tell a person exactly what to do under any situation that can arise in the game.
Supplementary angles	A pair of angles whose measures add to 180°. If two supplementary angles are adjacent, together they form a straight angle.
Term	(of an algebraic expression) A part of an algebraic expression, combined with other terms using addition or subtraction.
	Example: The expression $2x^2 + 3x - 12$ has three terms: $2x^2$, $3x$, and 12.
Term	(of a sequence) One of the items listed in a sequence.
	Example: In the sequence 3, 5, 7, . . . , the number 3 is the first term, 5 is the second term, and so on.
Theoretical probability	The likelihood of an event occurring, as explained by a theory or model, as distinct from **observed probability.**
Transversal	A line that intersects two or more other lines.

Example: The line *l* is a transversal that intersects the lines *m* and *n*.

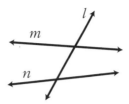

Trapezoid

A four-sided polygon with exactly one pair of parallel sides.

Example: Quadrilateral *PQRS* is a trapezoid, because $\overline{QR}$ and $\overline{PS}$ are parallel and $\overline{PQ}$ and $\overline{SR}$ are not parallel.

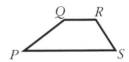

Triangle

A polygon with three sides.

Triangle inequality principle

The principle that the lengths of any two sides of a triangle must add up to more than the length of the third side.

Trigonometric function

Any of six functions defined for acute angles in terms of ratios of sides of a right triangle.

Vertex

(plural: **vertices**) See **Angle, Polygon,** and **Ray.**

Vertical angles

A pair of "opposite" angles formed by a pair of intersecting lines.

Example: Angles *F* and *G* are vertical angles.

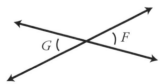

Whole number

A number that is either zero or a counting number.

x-intercept

A place on a graph where a line or curve crosses the *x*-axis.

y-intercept

A place on a graph where a line or curve crosses the *y*-axis.